BROKEN INTO PURPOSE

By Juquietta Witherspoon

Dedication

To God, the true author of my story.

Acknowledgements

One thing that my mother always told me is "You can't live in this world alone." She wasn't saying that my life would end along with everyone else's. What she meant was in life I would eventually come across situations that would require the help of others. With age comes wisdom and the older I get I understand why my mother thought it was so important to express that to me over and over again.

As you get into the chapters of this book you will read about a few of the people that did not allow me to live in this world alone...a few who literally saved my life and even more who contributed to my story in their own way. I am grateful for each and every one of you.

To my parents Joseph and Geneva, my story began with you. Although everything was not always krispy kreme, I would not be who I am today without the two of you. Being a parent myself now I understand how much you truly love and want the best for me.

Talayna and Trinty, my beautiful babies! I gave birth to you but you gave me life. You are my purpose! You give me every reason to go after my dreams. I'm thankful for the many times that God used the two of you to force me to get up off my butt and finish what I started.

And to my husband and bestfrind. You have been everything I needed! You are always my biggest supporter and I can not express enough how much that means to me. Writing this story was definitely a journey and you were right there experiencing the highs of completing each chapter, the lows of reliving tough moments and everything in between. This story is complete because of you. Our journey alone has been a rollercoaster but I am truly blessed to have you to take this ride with.

Authors Note

I never knew that writing a memoir would be so challenging yet rewarding. The idea to share my story started as a vision. I had no intentions of letting the world in on the things that I struggled with in my life, and in reality I was really afraid. I was afraid of judgement and also afraid of offending others. Until I realized that my story, was not only for me. There are so many others in the world that have fought the same battles I've fought, some maybe fighting those battles today.

I like to think of myself as a conquerer and if by sharing my struggles and strengths I can help others overcome theirs then my purpose will be fulfilled. Everything that I went through was designed to prepare me for my purpose. The stories shared in this book are my truth and while some may involve others, my intention is not to bash or bring shame to anyone. A part of my healing was learning to forgive and continue to love as God loves us. Enjoy!

Chapter 1

"Our hearts are much like our closets, if we keep packing things in there to hide them away instead of managing it the proper way, it is bound to burst open one day."

I hurried across the campus of Claflin University to avoid the scorching, hot sun beaming down the back of my neck. The ends of my hair were soaked with sweat and stuck to my skin like sadness after death. I remember thinking; *if I can only keep my feet from getting tangled up in these flip flops, I will be able to make it to my car and my AC.* That's when I saw a pair of shoes on the sidewalk heading in my direction and I looked up to avoid running into whoever they belonged to. This short guy was walking with his head tilted towards the ground as if he were looking for a break and I could tell his mind was clearly on something other than putting one foot in front of the other. He wasn't even aware that I was paying attention to him and his actions. I caught his eyes and smiled and said good morning. His face immediately transformed from worry to shock than his lips curved into a smile. After that very brief encounter, I realized how surprised he looked that someone cared enough to wish him a good morning. That was one of the *smallest* things I had ever done and it's amazing how it made me feel so *big* inside.

I often find myself people watching as I go about my day; not because I'm looking for flaws or looking for a potential date, but because people are more transparent with their feelings than they realize and I happen to be one of those observant people who pay close attention to others. Some people look as if they have it all together on the outside, but deep down there is an unspoken pain. There's no way to truly ever tell what someone is going through by just looking at them and for that reason, I make it my business to smile and give a warm greeting to everyone I cross paths with. I understand that for some, my greeting may be the brightest moment of their day.

I had no clue what that man was going through or what he was facing, but I knew in that moment; even if just for a split-second, I gave him something to smile about. It maybe because I am one of those people who smile through the hidden pain I can recognize others who do the same. Although we try to hide what we are going through inside, there are always moments when we slip up and our truth shows on our faces. Our hearts are much like our closets, if we keep packing things in there to hide them away instead of managing it the proper way, it is bound to burst open one day.

I'm sure the man thought no one was paying attention to his face, but I recognized that blank look of the worry, stress, depression and unhappiness. I recognized it because there were many days that I stood in my mirror, staring at the same look on my own face. I would stare for minutes in the mirror trying to convince myself that I was happy with what I saw staring back at me; tried to see for myself what so many others saw in me, but I couldn't see it because I lacked the confidence in myself to see anything other than a shy, awkward girl with flaws who didn't fit in with the other girls my age.

"You're so beautiful." I didn't see it when I looked in the mirror. "You're so smart, you've got a bright future ahead of you and you're so humble, too." I heard these compliments very often and each time I'd say under my breath, "I wish people would stop saying things they don't mean just to be nice." I just couldn't seem to see past my perceived flaws and shortcomings. I knew I would never be bold enough to go after my dreams…to do big things with my life and it was easier for me to accept that than it was to believe the kind things other people said about me.

At the age of 10, my perception of not fitting in was reinforced when I was fitted for my dance costume. Because I was roughly a half foot taller and 30 lbs heavier than the other dancers my age, the teachers told me that I would be in a different *size* category than the rest of the dance team.. I guess it made sense, because by the time I was 10 years old, I was already the size of an average 13-year-old girl; standing at 5'1"and weighing just over 100lbs, there was no way I was going to fit in with my 4'5", 72lbs friends on my dance team.

My parents sat me down to have a conversation with me about what I would have to do differently because of the transitions my body was going through. The old metal bunk bed that my brother and I shared creaked as I sat and shifted my body uncomfortably as they spoke. Outside the window beside the bed that looked out onto the front yard, I could hear my brother and cousins laughing and playing on the trampoline. "You call that a front flip...?" My brother laughed teasing one of my cousins.

My parents stood in front of me, each waiting for the other to start talking. They reminded me of the movie *Honey We Shrunk Ourselves*. If only I could shrink myself as tiny as the actors had in the movie, it would make it easier for me to hide. My father spoke first "You know you're not going to be able to play with little boys as much as you have been." I didn't understand what he meant. He was the one who had signed me up to play with boys in community sports before they got girls teams, and now he was telling me there was a problem with me playing with them. My mother explained, "Your body is beginning to develop now and that means your lady parts are more noticeable. Boys get curious and start asking questions then, they'll want to touch. It is important that you let someone know if anyone ever touches you in a way that is uncomfortable. No one should ever touch your lady parts that are considered bad touching." I stared at my hands, pinching the skin on knuckles. When my mother shifted the subject from touching to talk about how I am supposed to take care of my hygiene during my period, I wanted to cry. I was uncomfortable with my father hearing that.

    I gazed out the window at the other kids who were playing and not worrying about any of the confusing changes I was currently dealing with, and I just wanted to go outside and play, too. I just wanted to be a little girl. Although I appreciated my parents for educating me and taking the time to explain all of the changes that I was facing, because otherwise I would've been a mess, it was uncomfortable to be a child with a *grown-up* body. When I played with my friends, strangers looked at me like I was too old to be playing with the kids that were *actually* my age and it was embarrassing that my clothes were so much more mature than theirs because I could no longer shop in the kid's section.

Outside of the embarrassment and not fitting in with my friends anymore, there was a much deeper reason why my early development made me so uncomfortable. Men didn't look at me like I was a fourth grader in elementary school anymore, but unfortunately, even before I looked like a teenager, I learned that just being born a girl, made me vulnerable to sexual predators.

As is normal with many southern Black families, my parents did not allow me to stay at everyone's house. They only trusted family members to watch after me because as they always said, "Girls should not be from one house to the next." I don't think they ever really thought about family being sexual predators and they never allowed me to stay at my friend's houses. Only family and family wouldn't do something like that. It was their way of protecting me. I am grateful that my parents sat me down and had those uncomfortable conversations with me when they did because it was how I could distinguish good touch from bad touch; although it was four years too late.

As kids I was taught to believe that I can trust family members and that my older cousins are to look after the younger ones. That is exactly what I did, at the age of 6 I trusted anyone that was family and I looked to all my older cousins to protect me; but I learned not everyone is the same. There are some cousins who would protect every hair on my head and then there are others who made me want to pull every hair on my head out.

When I was 6, I would go to my great aunt's house to play with my cousins on the weekends. One of my older, male cousins always, would shower me with so much love and attention…sometimes, too much attention. He was about 9 or 10 years older than I was. He would always say that I was his *baby* and offer me treats to lure me in his room. "I got some candy, come and give your big cousin a hug." I would go to his room expecting to give a quick hug and collect my candy, but he always pushed the door closed when I walked in. *Why does he need to close the door to give me candy?* My 6-year old brain wondered, but my 6-year-old-self wanted the candy…so I stayed.

I wasn't comfortable, but I *really* wanted that candy! I looked around the room hoping to spot the candy he said he had, but all I saw was his messy room and dirty clothes all over the floor. His room smelled like fresh-cut musty onions and old, sweaty socks. He jumped on the bed pulling me along with him. "Where is the candy?" I asked trying to wiggle from his tight grasp around my upper body. "You got to give me my hug first." I didn't like the way his voice said the words. It was too low and rough. He was already holding me in a bear hug so I was unable to move my arms. I continued to struggle…trying to wiggle my way out of his tight hold, but I didn't make much progress. He was bigger than me, stronger than me and I was scared. He removed one arm to reach down to rub between my legs and tightened his grip on the other arm still around my body so that I could not get loose. I kicked as much as I could and cried for him to let me go. "Quietta!" someone yelled from the other room. He quickly let me go and yelled back "She's in here. she's coming." I went to another room climbed in the bed, placed the cover over my head and fell asleep. It was how I knew how to escape scary situations. I knew when I awoke my parents would be there to get me. It was one of many times he abused my innocence.

When others were present, he disguised the abuse as playful tickle fights. After my parents had the talk about good touch and bad touch with me, I knew what my cousin had been doing was not a *good touch* and I also knew I had to tell. The more my body developed, so did my fear of people who might touch me in bad ways.

My confidence diminished and I questioned if something was wrong with me. It was hard for me to express myself to my parents or anyone else about how I felt; so, I kept my feelings bottled in and tried to deal with them myself. It wasn't because my parents wouldn't have understood that made it hard for me to go to them with my issues, it was because they were always having issues of their own.

Up until I was 8 years old, my brother, Josh and I had a decent relationship with our parents; however, as tension and anger rose in our parents' relationship, our home environment became less than comfortable. We later found out the cause of the tension was my father's infidelity.

My mom, my brother and I were sitting in the living room watching t.v. The phone rang. I could hear my mother's conversation. "What do you mean he has a 2-year-old and one on the way?!" She looks as if she had just heard someone she loved died suddenly. "No, this isn't Joe's father's number; this is actually *his number.*" She didn't say too much as the person on the other end of the phone continued to explain. By the time she hung up, tears were flowing down her cheeks. She turned to my brother and me, we was both facing her curious to know what was going on. "Well, y'all have two little sisters now." My mother's voice was void of emotion. Josh and I exchanged looks...both of us too confused to respond. She walked passed us and locked herself in the bathroom. For hours, she cried while my brother and I stood at the bathroom door crying with her. The news caused a major divide in our household, but our parents decided to stay together. They didn't make the time to notice the fact I was suffering and withdrawing from them and my brother, to some degree. I didn't feel comfortable bothering them with how I felt, considering the difficult time they were going through.

    Josh and I had different ways of coping and living in the stressful and chaotic environment; on top of that, I had to find a way to cope with the abuse happening to me at the hands of my older cousin. While I retreated further into myself. my brother started acting out in school and hanging out with the wrong crowd. He was always angry; punching holes in the walls and raising his voice at my mom, blaming her for my dad's choices. His behavior demanded my parents' attention and that meant my parents ignored my needs. No one cared about how the stress, chaos and *abuse* affected me. I was cautious with my words and who I talked to... then *quiet*, was just who I was. Keeping sadness, anger and depression bottled up inside me, made me an overly emotional person and even now as an adult, I am still learning the proper ways of dealing with my emotions.

Despite my personal struggles; I continued to participate in activities and sports just like other kids in my community, but even when I was surrounded with fun and excitement I was lonely and alone. I locked myself in the bathroom and stared in the mirror thinking to myself how ugly I was how I wasn't like the other kids and how I didn't fit in. Nobody knew. Nobody understood. Nobody cared.

As my feeling of self-hatred, anger and depression continued to fester, so did my feeling of resentment towards my father. The drastic change in my relationship with him was not a one-way street. He didn't care much about me or how what he did and said hurt me. It seemed to me like my father felt we were not good enough. He had plans to leave us to create a new family as if we meant nothing to him. It got to the point he would do and say whatever he could to intentionally hurt me. There are scars that will never be seen and those are the ones that hurt the most. My father used his words like weapons designed to seek and destroy my self-esteem. The most brutal verbal attack launched by my father came in the form of six simple words, "I don't care about your feelings." I was at least 12 years old when my father shared this nugget of wisdom with me...the words wouldn't have hurt so badly if his actions didn't back them up.

My father, the one man that's supposed to protect me even if no one else does, was the very man that sent me to school, on more than one occasion, with evidence of his displeasure with me in the form of his full hand-print and knots on my face.

One such occasion was when my siblings and I were home alone one summer day. I was in the kitchen making hot dogs for everyone. My sister's, the two he had with another woman, said they did not want anything to eat at the time. A few minutes later, as I was fixing food for my brother, cousin and myself; my father walked in. "Did you make those girls hot dogs too." He accused. It was supposed to be a question, but it felt more like a statement. "Yes, I did, but they said they didn't want any right now." I replied. "Fix them some hot dogs right now! How are you going to make everybody else in the house hot dogs and leave them out?" I turned away from the stove with the fork in my right hand to face the voice that made my heart race with a mixture of fear and confusion. As he continued his tirade, my face continued to broadcast my anger, hurt and bewilderment. "I wasn't leaving them out. I asked them and they said they didn't want any--I" Before I could finish my sentence, I was struck in the face. The slap took my breath away. I stood there in disbelief, trying desperately to hold in my tears. "Oh, you think you scare me?" He asked. Again...and a few more times I took hits to the face. He grabbed me by the arms jerking me around, causing my body to collide with the kitchen cabinets. The physical pain didn't hurt as much as the pain in my heart. My father chose to create a bigger gap in our relationship the day he left me bruised and confused in our kitchen...he seemed all right with his decision, but I was left without a father or a reason why.

    I knew most of the dysfunction in my family stemmed from his choices, which caused us pain he didn't care to heal. At the time, I didn't realize even though he made poor decisions that broke me, he would never be the one to heal the pain he planted inside me. I had to go to God and forgive my choices, his choices and then move on. I was too young and too hurt to understand back then.

    During a heated conversation with my father when I was just entering middle school, he asked me did I hate him, and my answer was yes. I never *really* hated my father, I only wanted his love. At the time of that conversation, I was very hurt. My father did not care about our family and I stopped expecting anything from him. I didn't hate him, I hated his choices. I hated that he was too selfish to think about how his actions would affect us. I hated that his plans were to leave us like we meant nothing to him. Imagine being a kid carrying personal hurt as well as the hurt of your mother and brother. That emotional weight followed me and got much heavier as I grew older.

My difficult relationship with my father only added to my self-hatred. *How could I love me if the man that created me didn't?* When I was about five years old I was very much a daddy's girl, now I no longer had my father's love. I still loved my dad and I needed him to care about me, as well. Through the years there were many times I tried to restore the bond we had or at least engage in a meaningful conversation with him, but each time, I was disappointed. He had no interest in knowing me, because honestly, he didn't have a clue who I really was. The first man I soaked my pillow at night for was my own father. I've lamented the lack of a relationship with my father. I mean, really! I grew up in his household but I did not have a place in his heart. At the age of 14, I had not learned to truly forgive. Eventually, I learned about forgiveness as my relationship grew with God. I learned that sometimes we must forgive people who never told us they were sorry. I also learned that forgiveness was not for him, but for me.

Before I learned the lesson of forgiveness; I had just mastered going from elementary school and one teacher all day to my middle school days with eight different teachers. So...my forgiveness for my father would have to wait a little longer. Maybe it is *forgiveness* that is best served cold...I don't know, but he would get it when he got it and not a moment sooner! From elementary to middle school, the most difficult challenge was keeping my mind intact. I fought daily to convince myself of two truths; I was happy and I loved me.

One thing about depression is some days I felt fine and other days I felt the weight of the world was on my shoulders. It was a rainy Saturday morning and my little sister's Jana and Javonne and I were sitting in the living room. I was watching TV and they were playing with dolls. Because my parents had stayed together and decided to try and make their marriage work, the girls became a part of our lives. I was 14 years old and my sisters 6 and 5; so, on the weekends they visited I was sometimes left in charge of watching them while our parents worked. My brother Josh and our cousin, Martel; who was also like a brother to us, were in Josh's bedroom playing the video game. I don't know how the walls and windows were not destroyed as my sisters used their dolls and their high-pitched voices to remodel the living room.

"Y'all be quiet I'm trying to watch TV" I demanded. They got quiet for a second and went right back to being loud again.

"Let those kids play, Quietta. They are not bothering you." My brother yelled from his room. "I'm trying to watch TV and I can't hear with all that noise." Already aggravated, I screamed at my sisters "I said be quiet! I'm trying to watch TV...now let me say it again and I'm gonna pop y'all and take those dolls." Feeling like their mama, but not really.

"No, you won't!" My brother said, walking from his room. "I said leave those girls alone. If you want to bully somebody, bully me." *Bullying? He was ready to fight me because I threatened to pop them for not listening.* "Hit them and I'll hit you" I had no intention of harming them in any way and I was shocked my brother, who was always the one that was on my side, was standing toe to toe with me with his fist clenched. Threatening to punch me in my face. My siblings and I are very close and very protective of each other, when he accused me of bullying them, I felt horrible about myself because I would never do anything to hurt any of them in any way and the thought of me making them feel mistreated made me feel sad.

My brother was always overly protective of me, even though it was quite annoying and embarrassing sometimes; I always appreciated him for that because I knew that he truly cared. But that day he was the one who was threatening to hurt me and all because he did not agree with me yelling at *them*. He was always the one who would comfort me when I cried and tell me everything would be okay. In that moment, he didn't care about me either. Maybe it was just that I was emotional, but I got tired of feeling like I didn't matter to anyone.

After arguing with my brother, I grabbed the biggest knife that I could find and ran and locked myself in the bathroom. I sat on the toilet crying my eyes out. I no longer wanted to be a burden to any of my family by continuing to exist, but I didn't know how to end it. I thought hard about the fastest and easiest way to use the knife to kill myself. There was no point in living anymore. Everyone's life would be better if I took my own. I had to act before someone came in. My entire body shook with every thump of my heart. Tears streamed down my face, I squeezed the knife in my right hand with white-knuckle force and moved it infinitesimally toward my left wrist. Hands still shaking. Seconds and minutes became weeks and months as I placed the knife on my wrist. In that moment, I decided I would not be afraid anymore; no longer afraid of the loneliness, the sadness and the lack of love. I wanted to cut my wrist, sit and watch as the blood poured from my arm...until I could no longer feel the pain. There was a loud bang outside the door and it flew open, Martel rushed in, his face was a slab of anger. He didn't say anything as he pried the knife out of my hands. He looked at me, a wall of fury and turned around to leave the bathroom. *I have no idea how he even knew what I was up to.* I sat there, crying and angry that he stopped me, but I am eternally grateful he cared enough to save my life.

Spoonful of Wisdom

That night when my mother got word of what happened, she and I went to her sister's house. Feeling completely numb and dazed, I sat in silence listening to the two of them talk about what could possibly have made me want to take my own life. I watched as my mother broke down in tears. I was disappointed in myself for making her feel she hadn't given me a good enough life to want to live. Knowing I made my mother feel guilty in some way, only made me feel worse about myself.

It wasn't long before my father got word of what happened. He called my aunt's house and talked to both she and my mother before asking to speak with me. I placed the phone to my ear, not knowing what to expect, still in a daze I forced out a weak hello. There was a part of me that was hoping that my father would show that he cared, it would've helped to hear the same comforting words that my mom and aunt gave me, come from his mouth. However, what I got was the exact opposite. He yelled at me how I must've gone crazy and I was stupid for trying to kill myself. He accused me of doing it all for attention. My dad was completely clueless to assume I did what I did for attention. How could he not see my pain? The words dripped like acid on my already burning heart. I didn't want to burden my mom, I couldn't talk with my dad, but I knew I needed to talk to someone.

I wasn't comfortable speaking to a stranger about what I was going through, but my aunt and my mom knew I needed guidance. That meeting changed my life for the better. When my aunt introduced me to the counselor the first thing I noticed was the small gray hairs that stuck out of his mustache. He was short and shrunken by old age. I immediately thought, great, grandpa here is going to lecture and judge me. Instead he was thoughtful and serene. He didn't judge me at all. He told me stories of when he once attempted to hurt himself and how it turned out. He explained how he once tried to amputate his toe by sitting his bare feet on a stump and taking a hammer to his big toe because he was upset with someone else. He laughed and said that he will never try that fool break again because it only got him a trip to the ER and made him the butt of a lifetime of embarrassing jokes. He was the last person I thought would get a laugh out of me during that time, but after talking to him for only a few minutes I was comfortable.

He told me of God's love for me and the importance of me being here if God needed me here. I left the first appointment with him, a brand-new person. I started to feel much better about myself. Before meeting with him, I knew of God but didn't know God for myself. I accepted God's love for me and in turn I realized my love for Him. I wanted an intimate relationship with Him. Every day after that appointment and still even today, his words continue to replay in my head. I lost contact with him, but I wish I would have kept in touch with him or could even remember his full name. If I could speak to him today, I would tell him just how much he helped to change my life.

Our society and our culture tell us if we ever need counseling, then obviously we are crazy. They teach us we don't need counseling for certain situations, that everything can be handled in other ways. Depression is real. Mental illness is real. Anxiety is real. Someone who doesn't have to fight that battle cannot begin to understand what it feels like. Yes, there is no problem too big for God, but we must recognize why God created people with certain gifts. If there is ever a time that you feel like you need help please go get the help because it could literally save and change your life. I was amazed at how much I had learned, how it changed so much in me, and how good it made me feel to express so much of what I had kept bottled in for so long. You'll find in this book there were and still are difficult days, when I struggle to go on, but if I would've never gotten the help I needed...I would not be where I am today. After learning of God's unconditional love for me during that counseling session, I finally realized what was missing between my father and me.

~Prayer~

Dear God,

As a child, I struggled with loving who you created me to be. I did not understand the importance of my existence. It was hard for me to see that my life had any meaning. It was when I found you that I knew that my living was not in vain. My prayer is that you will help me be who and what I needed in those days that I struggled to like myself and when I feel like no one cares. I give thanks to you for leading me to the help I need and the lessons I'll learn in the process.

_____

_____

_____

_____

_____

_____

_____

_____

Chapter 2

"We don't always learn our lesson when God is showing us signs about people or situations. Sometimes it takes heartbreak and disappointment for us to listen."

"And your new 2008 Homecoming Queen is Miss. Juquietta McFadden!" It was my senior year and last chance to participate in Homecoming court. I stood there as stiff as a board for a minute, with that pageant girl grin still on my face feeling like I must have just been imagining them call my name. "Go girl that's you." My cousin Dedrick, who was my escort, said pushing me towards the front. It wasn't just my imagination. I had just been announced the new homecoming queen. That is my most memorable moment of High school. High school years were my fun years. I was always surrounded by a group of friends that brought mostly laughter and joy wherever we went. We did almost everything together, from band trips to eating lunch, and activities during and after school hours. When I was around my friends, I could forget about some of my troubles at home. I entered high school when situations in my life were still rocky, there was still chaos in my family, my relationship with my father was still deteriorating, and I was still dealing with mental illness. However, I was getting older and learning to accept that life wasn't and probably never would be perfect. Life and experience came together with precision to ensure I had opportunities to continue to learn lessons to move me towards my purpose.

I stayed busy in school because it kept me from thinking about what was going on at home.

Not only did I have my friends and activities to keep my mind off the chaos within my family, but I had a steady boyfriend of 3 years to help keep my mind off my home and family life. We started dating my seventh-grade year and he was in the eighth. He gave me the attention I no longer received from my father and that attention made me feel special in a way that even my father's love and attention couldn't. He wasn't my family, which means he didn't have to love me, but he did.

A part of me knew that things were not as good as they seemed, but I didn't want to accept the reality that I was not as special as he made me feel. However; week after week, rumors about him and other girls surfaced. I couldn't understand why the men in my life continued to reject me and the love I gave them. I couldn't see myself with anyone but him. My excitement and joy revolved around him and us and what we did when we were together. I saw him in passing and my heart tripped over itself like clumsy feet, but it was the best fall I ever took. He made me laugh when all I wanted to do was cry...he was my perfect escape. We talked on the phone from the time we got home from school until one of us fell asleep...I can't believe I willingly gave up my sleep just to talk to him, but I did. He was my best friend and we were the couple that others tried to emulate. I wanted to marry him. I had a vision of our lives after high school and I didn't want my vision ruined. Hindsight is 20/20. If I could go back and give my high school-self a piece of advice, I would tell me, "You are worth more than you know and not every vision is meant to come to fruition." I knew I gave love, attention, and support to our relationship and to him; however, as I look back I'm not sure he was giving as much as I was.

    I willingly gave him my mind, my heart, and even my body; but it was still not enough, in the end, to keep his eyes and hands from wandering. Although he never pressured me; because I didn't want to lose our relationship, I decided to have sex with him. If I gave myself to him in that way he would see I really cared about him and choose only me. There were many other girls willing to do what I wasn't doing, and even if the rumors weren't true, I was lame for not doing it. Why in the world would I think myself a lame for not doing what everyone else was doing is beyond me, but back then...it was how I felt. I convinced myself I was ready because I really loved him. We talked about it many times before it happened and even after I had sex with him, the rumors didn't stop.

"I tried to hurry out before you left." He said.

"You know I was going to wait on you anyway," I said blushing.

"You going straight home when you leave?" He asked.

"Yeah. Where else am I supposed to go?" I deadpanned.

"Well, you could come to my house." He said biting his lips and twisting his head slightly to the right. I knew what he was thinking.

"Umm...if Trina is okay with driving that far then I'll come." I knew she would be down to go wherever I wanted or needed to go. I was not worried about getting home too late because I knew my parents trusted me and they knew if I got home late, it meant practice went late or I was hanging out. I told Trina about the plans and just as I expected, she was all for it. I rode with him and she followed behind.

    The drive to his house, which was only about 15-20 minutes away, was like driving across country. What in the world am I thinking? With my luck, we'll get in an accident and my parents will find out that I was somewhere that I wasn't supposed to be. I tried to look comfortable, but based on the light shivers running through my frozen body and the sweat slicking my palms, I was anything but comfortable. He sang along and turned up the radio to Pretty Rickey's, *Grind on Me*. I suddenly wanted to turn around and go back home. I wasn't ready for what I knew was about to happen. I need more time to think this over. But this was the guy I loved and I didn't want to disappoint him. I prayed silently, Lord please don't let me get caught.

    We arrived to his house and got out of the car. We stood outside a few minutes talking to my best friend and my boyfriend's brother. He grabbed my hand and led me in the house. He told his brother to "Holla or something if someone comes." Once in his room, he ensured me everything was going to be okay. He was gentle, we were safe and everything was just how I imagined, but it hit me that I could not take back what was happening. My parents would be so disappointed. I was disappointed... 15, unwed and not thinking about the consequences of my actions. I stared at the popcorn ceiling, as silent raindrops trickled down my cheeks. My virginity was gone.

    After the first time; the summer became more about sex than band, cheerleading or football. By the start of my tenth-grade year, we were both hooked. I disappointed myself every time I made the choice and skipped school or after school activities to be with him. I realized my choices did not reflect my true desires, but what kept me going back was how sweet he was to me and the hope that it wouldn't matter since we would be married someday. I didn't realize what I was experiencing was a soul tie. A soul tie is when two souls form a link through an intimate and emotional bond. The most common way soul ties are created is through repetitive sexual activity with the same individual. The bond formed by a soul tie is designed to produce a productive and healthy relationship between a husband and wife as noted in Matthew 19:5, "And said, For this cause shall a man leave father and mother, and shall cleave to his wife: and they twain shall be one flesh."

In this soul tie, my soul was empty without him. He was the only thing I thought about. I went to sleep thinking about him, dreamt about him constantly, and woke up thinking about him. When I tried to move on from our relationship, it didn't work because nothing else felt right without him. A soul tie cannot be broken easily. What I didn't know is that it was important to guard my spirit from certain things and people because it is easy to get attached to someone but much harder to break the attachment. It took intensive prayer, renouncing of the ties, and repenting of my disobedience.

It wasn't just the soul tie that had me stuck in a negative relationship, I was addicted to hearing him tell me how much he loved me and how beautiful and special I was to him. I knew my parents loved me, but I didn't hear it as often as I wanted from them. Hearing those words from my boyfriend every day was what I needed. When I was I was sure my dad could not care less about me, his words were enough to let me know he did.

Even though we broke up my senior year, I still called on him when I didn't want to or I couldn't deal with the hurt and chaos taking place in my life and he was always there. He never told me to go away or that he was too busy; however, his willingness to be there for me made it impossible for me to accept we were done. I was dependent on the love and the bond we had. My dependency on him diminished as my relationship with God grew. It is only as I continue to deepen my relationship with God that I gained an understanding of just how much my relationship with him cost me.

Time and sleep are what I needed. Being tied to the wrong soul is exhausting and those are the only two assets one can't recover. Even a broken heart will heal over time, but time and sleep cannot be recouped. I did; however, gain a clearer perspective. I realized that I was more in love with him than he was with me. Although it was a slap in the face, it helped me to move on.

It was the summer after I graduated high school. I spent Sunday morning in church thinking of what I could do once church ended. I came up with nothing. I sat on the front porch in the rocking chair gazing at the beautiful. blue skies filled with silent clouds that looked like lavender. The cool breeze from the trees was perfect. The day was too beautiful to waste sitting in the house, so I decided to call the one person I knew would answer and would be willing to entertain me. We had officially been broken up for about 4 or 5 months. Although we were not a couple, we still got together to hang out and sometimes have sex. My choice to continue seeing him and being with him sexually was intensified by the soul tie we shared and in turn, the soul tie we shared was intensified by our continual sexual activity. He invited me over, just as I knew he would. I wonder if he dealt with the same struggle of letting me go as I was dealing with at the time?

When I arrived at his house, he greeted me with a hug and a kiss as he always did. Nothing felt different about our relationship...it was just like we were still together. I sat on the edge of the bed so he wouldn't think I only came to have sex. He laid across the bed, we talked and shared some laughs about random things. We were both enjoying each other's company when he suddenly got up and hurried out of the room with a worried look on his face. Apparently, he heard a familiar car pulling into his yard. When he came back into the room he said to me in what was almost a whisper but it was clear by the tone of his voice that he was kicking me out "You gotta go, my girlfriend outside!" He must be joking because I know he didn't just say his girlfriend was outside. I sat for a second waiting for him to say he was joking. "Did you hear me? You. Got. To. Go!" He whisper-screamed in a louder, more forceful tone than before. "Go to the back room with my cousin or get in the closet of something until she leaves. "He demanded. I looked from left to right, there must be somebody else sitting in this room because there was no way he was trying to get me to run around his house hiding from another girl. The shock from his words just left me unable to move anything but the muscles in my face. I stood there looking at him in disbelief. He repeated "You gotta go!" My heart felt a little bit of everything at that moment. I was shocked that he was treating me like I was some random chick and angry that he was trying to get me to hide as if I had no respect for myself or relationships.

Hindsight really is 20/20. I believed I held myself to a higher standard, when in all honesty; I was just a girl who didn't respect myself enough to walk away from a boy who used me. Self-respect and self-love go together and there can't be one without the other. It hurt me, though. I had never heard him call anybody else his girlfriend. He had moved on and I was still stuck. Although I was destroyed emotionally, I still had my dignity, at least enough not to hide someone's closet and I was *definitely* not about to run through this man's house trying to hide from another woman. Instead, I walked through the living room straight out the front door--passing his girlfriend along the way. She was very calm because she had just seen me walk out of her man's bedroom. Her eyes caught mine as I walked pass and she gave a friendly smile and shifted to the right to allow me to exit. I shook my head and walked out, still in disbelief. She clearly did not know who I was or that he and I had been in a relationship for years and were still together in many ways. I heard him greet her with a loving "Hey baby..." Adding insult to injury for me.

I was so disappointed in myself. Even though I had not intentionally done anything to hurt her, I knew I had to take responsibility for my part in the ordeal. If the relationship had truly ended, I would not have allowed myself to be treated like I was nothing more than a random hookup I knew for sure my feelings for him were far deeper than his feelings for me. He treated me like I meant absolutely nothing to him and it was almost as if he enjoyed the moment when he kicked me out because his girlfriend came over. I felt guilty for being at his house when he had a girlfriend. I thought about how I would've felt if I had found another girl at his house when we were dating. I would never want to cause another person that kind of pain.

Shortly after leaving his house, he called. After ignoring the first few calls, I decided to answer to see what he had to say. "You okay?" He asked. I wasn't okay. Deep down I was blindsided and even more hurt with the way he treated me; however, I did not want him to know how hurt I was because I didn't want him to know how much I still cared for and about him. "I promise I didn't know that she was coming bae. She was supposed to be at work." Everything he said went in one ear and out the other. Nothing he said justified his actions. "Can you please come back?" He asked. "Come back!" I said sardonically. "After the *way* you just treated me...you don't have to ever worry about me coming to your house ever again." Sitting in the car in Wal-Mart's parking lot, tears made my eyes burn as I flung my hurt towards him over the phone. I hung up the phone before the tears could drop. I made myself get out of the car, go to the store to get the toy I promised my mom I would get for my little sister if she let me use the car.

I didn't expect him to disrespect his girlfriend by keeping me there; I didn't even know there was a girlfriend until I was being put out of his house. Although I was still very much attached to him emotionally, spiritually and of course...physically, the separation and the memory of that encounter helped break the soul tie we shared. We don't always learn our lesson when God is showing us signs about people or situations. Sometimes it takes heartbreak and disappointment for us to listen.

Spoonful of Wisdom

One of the reasons why I caused myself the heartache I did by dealing with someone outside of marriage is because I was seeking the love and attention that only God can really give. Not even my mother or father could ever fill the void of God's love. My ex-boyfriend and I were both young and trying to live adult lives, not knowing what we were getting ourselves into. I didn't know what God had planned for my life, but I knew he had other plans for both of us. We made a choice to engage in activity that God meant for husband and wife. The consequences we had to deal with was a result of our disobedience. We expected too much from a relationship better suited for friendship than romantic love. God was leading me down a different road and that meant some thoughts, habits, and people had to be released for me to stay on track. To put me on the right path, my mom sat me down and talked to me about bad touch and good touch and hygiene, but I wish she would have talked to me about relationships and first love. My parents started dating in middle school and I watched as my mom tied herself in knots to my dad, but her hold on him was tenuous at best. I almost continued the cycle of being bound to a man who couldn't value me, but thank God, the ties were broken. Looking back at the relationship between both my parents and my ex-boyfriend and myself, it is obvious to me now that being tied to the wrong person drained the joy, peace, energy, and motivation from me.

After recognizing the negative soul tie which existed between my ex and myself, it became easy to see the negative soul tie that existed within my relationship with my father, as well. It didn't matter how many times my father showed me who he was and what I meant to him, I tried for years to reestablish a connection with him because I wanted a better relationship. I was exhausted and weakened from tying myself to the negativity that flowed between us. Even today, my father and I don't have the relationship I wanted for us because I decided that I was no longer interested in being the only one trying to maintain a relationship...so, I let it be whatever it will be. So, you can see that soul ties are not just formed between two people that are physically intimate. Soul ties can be a link with anyone who you have an emotional connection with.

~Prayer~

Dear God,

I thank you for loving me unconditionally. I pray you will never allow me to seek the love only you can give me in any one else. Forgive me for my mistakes Father. Loosen any ungodly ties that were not ordained by you. Help me to focus on you and the love you have for me. Whenever you see fit for me to be in a relationship, send the person that you have just for me and help me to know when it is real.

_____

_____

_____

_____

_____

_____

_____

_____

_____

_____

Chapter 3

"I was never going to be the party girl known for drinking, smoking and having sex with anything that moved; it was not my personality and I was not going to let anyone talk me into losing who I was just to fit in with everyone else."

The lessons I learned during my four years of high school did not all come from teachers, books, and projects. The most important lessons were learned at the hands of family, friends and a boyfriend; they all taught me about myself and helped me see the kind of person I wanted to be. Those lessons are the ones that gave me the courage to choose to attend an out-of-state college when the time came to do so. After graduating high school, I wanted to go far away from my hometown in hopes of not having to be reminded of any of the negative experiences. I wanted a new city, new experiences, and new people; I could have a new start and begin to enjoy my life a little more. I thought by moving away from home, I could continue to avoid the issues of depression, insecurity and loneliness I hid behind my mask. Running away from my pain didn't work because the root of the problem was within me, so wherever I went they followed me and would be there until I figured out how to deal with them.

  My father thought I could get the same education closer to home; however, despite my father's opinion of me going to a school out of state, I began my first semester of college at Johnson C. Smith University in Charlotte, North Carolina. This college wasn't my first choice, but it was the only college I actually visited; granted the visit was years before I would be ready for college. This first visit was when my church, along with other area churches, chose to take a group of girls to visit JCSU as a part of a college tour. My first impression of this school was fun, successful

Black people. I wasn't sure if I wanted to go to four-year college; therefore, I procrastinated filling out the applications. Because I waited so long to decide where I wanted to go...JCSU is where I found myself in the fall of 2008

Johnson C. Smith offered me everything I wanted: the new city, new experiences and new friends; however, I still did not find the peace I sought. Even though I was surrounded by people, I was still not a part of the people. I didn't fit in or at least, I didn't see me fitting in. I was there physically, but I had no joy. It was the first time I had been so far away from my family and the place I always called home. I was homesick and once again, depression became a part of my life. The only time I spent outside of my room was to attend classes, eat and study. Between classes, I called my mother, no matter how many classes I had a day. Talking to her made the days feel shorter.

"Hey Ma, what are y'all doing? Where is Layshia." I spoke into my phone as I walked across campus.

"She's still asleep, you just getting out of class?" She asked. My mother knew my class schedule almost as well as me.

"Yeah, I'm about to head back to the room until the next one." I didn't want her to worry about me, but I didn't know what else to do.

"Okay. You alright? Why you sound so down?" My mom's questions fell from her lips like drops of rain hitting a tin roof.

"I'm okay...still kind of tired, but do you think you will be able to come get me this weekend, Ma? I really want to come home." I tried hard not to cry talking to her, but every time I thought about the possibility of having to spend the weekend on campus, caused liquid fear to slither through my belly like worms in a bait can.

"Well...I will try my best, but I ain't making no promises."

Staying on campus during the week was enough for me. On the weekends, I wanted to be home so I could spend time spoiling my baby sister Jalayshia, who was only a toddler when I went off to college. She made me happy at a time in my life when little else could. I also used the weekends home to hang out with my cousins, Brittney and Dedrick, who also happened to be my best friends. The three of them brought me comfort, each in their own way. No one understood why I felt the way I did, everyone told me that I needed to just enjoy the college experience. Don't you think I would if I could, but I can't seem to make it happen?

On one of my weekend visits home, my cousin and I were in the car on the way to God knows where when she started asking me about college life.

"How is school going? Did you meet any cute guys yet?" My older cousin asked during one of our girl talk moments.

"It's going okay, and I've met cute guys, but none that I'm interested in."

"Girrrrl you better get out there and experience some of those college men, I'm telling you! You don't know what you're missing. Johnson C. Smith is a party school so I know those parties be epic ain't it?" Her excitement was another passenger in the car...riding shotgun right on top of me.

" I wouldn't know, I haven't been to any. I'm just not into all of that." I replied a little annoyed. Every time I talked to someone from home, they cared more about how the parties were and if I found a man yet than how I was doing mentally and academically. "I just like to have the type of fun that doesn't require me to be intoxicated or lower my standards." I hoped that would change the subject, but it didn't.

"Man. Girl you gonna miss out on the whole college experience if you don't get out there and enjoy those things. That's what college is about."

Well, excuse me for going to college to get an education.

There were others who constantly pressured me to drink or try drugs. I had never done anything like that in my life and I didn't think it would make me feel any better, anyway. I received the most pressure to sleep around, like being a ho was a part of the college experience I was missing out on by not putting myself out there. If those girls who wanted me to sleep with every boy on campus and the boys who wanted to be one of the boys I slept with only knew what I knew about sex, they would never be so reckless with themselves.

I was never going to be the party girl known for drinking, smoking and having sex with anything that moved; it was not my personality and I was not going to let anyone talk me into losing who I was just to fit in with everyone else. I hated being judged for not compromising who I was, but I knew enough to be proud of the fact that I didn't. The few friends I gained at JCSU, shared my likes and dislikes so we spent most of our time there together counting down the days until the end of the semester.

College life was already stressful enough for me when the unthinkable happened my depression multiplied tenfold and my world spiraled out of control. Every aspect of my life became too much for me to deal with. I was breaking and there was nothing I could do about it. One Friday afternoon my brother and a friend of his were on their way to take me home for the weekend. My brother was constantly calling to make sure that he had the right directions. "Hey Tootie, we're on the way to get you but ummm...we don't know exactly where we're going; so I will call you if we get lost." I shook my head as I responded to my brother. "Oh, Lord. Well if y'all get lost I can't do much for you."

I, along with hundreds of other students, was sitting in the auditorium awaiting the arrival of the celebrity producer and author, Mr. Fonzworth Bentley. It was my first time seeing anyone famous in person, so I was extremely excited and anxious. Mr. Bentley was already about 5 minutes late and my brother had already called a few times to make sure he was still on the right route. My friends and I were laughing, bouncing around, enjoying the wait. We were all excited that and even more so because it was Friday.

"Well, Mr. Bentley needs to come on now, what's taking him so long," I said anxiously.

"Right, he's trying to make a grand entrance, coming in fashionably late." Keyana laughed.

"Well wherever he's at, he needs to hurry up because I still have a class in a few minutes." One of my other friends said.

"Y'all? I don't think he's coming. He done stood us up, man." We all laughed when I realized that my brother was calling again. "Oh Lord, my brother is calling again, I bet they got lost." I joked. As soon as I answered the phone, I noticed that my brother's tone was much different from before. Josh is always loud and jokey, but the way he shouted through the phone in that moment was a clear indication what he was saying was not a joke.

"Quietta did you hear what just happened?"

"What happened?" I whispered trying not to bring too much attention to myself in the gym full of students. My heartbeat double timed as I waited for his response not knowing what to expect. "Brittney just died " He shouted with a little crackle in his voice. Brittney is a very common name. In fact, I had three Brittney's I was tight with.

"Which Brittney?" I asked not even giving a thought that it was the closest one to me, the one that I grew up having sleepovers every weekend with, the one I called my sister, my blood cousin who I talked to daily. I did not want to hear that it was her.

"Our Brittney." He shouted. His words poured like hot lava into my ears.

I had so many questions. How? Why? What Happened, Is this real? They all tried to come out in one sentence. Paralyzed by what I heard, I could not get my words to form. I quickly snatched the phone away from my ear and forcefully pressed the end call button as if I could undo the conversation, wishing I had not heard what came from the other end of the line. I sat breathless for a few seconds still in shock, eyes wide and staring straight ahead still unable to form words. My friends could tell whatever was said on the phone was not good.

"Quietta what's wrong? Everything okay?" They asked repetitively. I turned to Keyana, who knew Brittney.

"My Brittney died." My face and eyes burned and my entire body shook as the words spilled from my mouth. Everything seemed to be spinning in circles and suddenly I felt like I was in an empty room. I jumped up and ran out the double doors leading out of the auditorium...not noticing a single soul.

    I was weak as I opened the doors and the misty rain and reality hit me all at once. I staggered down the steep steps almost falling when my friends, who had followed me out of the auditorium, caught me. I felt my entire heart break and I could no longer hold back my pain. My friends walked me into the lobby area of my dorm building. The counselor was already there because another student in the building had just lost her grandmother. She told my friends to walk me up to my room and she would be there in just a minute. When I walked in the room the first picture I noticed on my bulletin board was a picture of myself, my best friend, Katrina, and my dear cousin Brittney from our senior prom only a few months before. It was like a fist to the chest. How could she be gone?

Still, in tears, I took the picture down and held it to my heart. I sat on my bed holding the picture close to the chest, rocking back and forth, crying uncontrollably. Keyana, who was also my roommate, stayed and tried to help calm me down until the counselor came.

When the counselor came in she took the picture from my hands. "Tell me about Brittney. What type of person was she? When was the last time you talked to her? What did you two last do together?" She asked in a soft nurturing tone. I was too distraught to tell her that Brittney was goofy, she laughed at any and everything or that she was the last person I talked to last night and that we had spent last weekend together shopping. As much as I tried, I couldn't control the tears. The muscles in my chest tightened and I felt a piercing pain and started to panic. I held my chest with both hands trying to breathe without it hurting.

The counselor took me by the hand, "Sweetie you have to calm down. You can't go home to your family when your brother arrives if you end up in the hospital yourself." I took deep breaths slowly until my breathing was fairly normal again. "That's it, you have to breathe. Do you need me to stay here with you?" She asked. I shook my head no. I wanted to be alone for a few minutes. She left after telling me to call if I needed her. When the counselor left, Keyana re-entered the room after stepping away to the bathroom. "You want to know what happened Quietta? During my time with the counselor, Keyana had stepped outside to answer a call that came into my phone from another cousin who was calling to see if I was alright. A few minutes later Keyana's boyfriend came to take her home for the weekend and I was alone. I called my mother and although I was hurt I was also angry that no one other than my brother called to tell me anything; I knew they didn't want either of us to find out while we were so far away and had to travel two hours back.

"Ma..."

"Hey, you left yet?" She asked as if nothing was wrong.

"Ma, what happened to Brittney?" I asked through sobs.

"Who told you?"

"What happened?" I asked again.

"...she passed." I could hear the strength that my mother was holding on to for me leave her voice. I could hear the family in the background, words of encouragement filtered through the phone

"God needed her more than we did."

"The good die young. We just have to be strong for each other. She wouldn't want us to cry ourselves sick."

Brittney's death was the heartbreak that finally broke me. I had no idea how I was going to get through that. Nothing made sense to me. She was so young and we always talked about what life would be like when we grow up. I was just talking to her the night before. I didn't understand why God called her home. She and I were always more like sisters. I, Brittney, and Dedrick were extremely close. We nicknamed ourselves the 3 musketeers. The two of them were the only family members that called, visited and expressed their love and appreciation for me regularly. Losing her was the hardest thing I ever faced. Life is truly unfair. Already dealing with so much mentally, it made me question my own life. I asked myself if I were called to leave this world now how would I be remembered. I also questioned how I could go on living my own life when someone else I love is gone. Why am I living? Why did God take her and not me? She deserved to live.

Spoonful of Wisdom

Talking about Brittney was difficult for a long time; until one day...it wasn't. Anyone who has ever lost someone they love knows the pain never really goes away, but it does eventually get better. This was a challenge I knew only God could help me overcome. After her passing, I still had to complete my first semester of college but I decided to be so far away from family only made it harder for me to heal. Not a day passed I didn't get emotional thinking about the things I wish she were here to see. During classes, my mind would drift from what the instructors were teaching about to memories of us as kids, growing into adults. I made it through Fall semester and decided I would transfer closer to home to attend Claflin University after Christmas break.

No matter where I went, it was still hard knowing I couldn't share my experiences with her. It was hard living. I often picked up the phone to call her out of habit to take a ride somewhere with me or just share a laugh with her. The reality that she was no longer available drove me deeper into depression. Reminders of her are everywhere, smells, and certain songs on the radio, holidays, and other things that once connected us. I saw her parents be as strong as they were that helped me to gain strength to go on as well. I never really thought about death much until I lost her, but I learned the reality is we all must leave this world at some point.

No one knows when they will be called, but everyone would surely be called someday. I grieved for so long it was hard for me to understand how everybody else could just go on with their lives after losing a loved one. When I spoke to her mother I knew if she could have the strength to get through burying her child and still find reasons to smile, I could too. Once I stopped questioning why God took her away and started remembering all of the good times we shared it became a bit easier to bear. Family encouraged me not rush the grieving process because everyone doesn't grieve the same.

I think about my own life. We aren't promised to live 100 years on this earth. Death doesn't have an age limit. I made the choice to enjoy my life. Most of my life was spent worrying, stressing, crying, and hating my own existence. I go to church more often because it helps me to heal and understand more about who God created me to be so I can enjoy my own life. I cried out to God many times and before I knew it I was crying tears of joy. I am grateful I experienced life and created memories with Brittney while she was here.

~Prayer~

Dear God,

Of all the emotional burdens, I had to bear in my life, this has been the worst. The pain of losing someone so close and dear to my heart has broken me down in so many ways. It hurts to know as I live I will never see her face again. I did not understand why you called her home but I know you needed her more than I. I realized I was not really living and making the most of my life. I pray you give me the strength to get through the days of missing her presence here in this world. I understand that death will come to each of us and we will not know the day or the hour, so I pray you help me to be prepared for when my time comes, but until then help me to live.

_____

_____

_____

_____

_____

_____

_____

_____

Chapter 4

"It became clear that it wasn't that I didn't fit in, it was that I didn't know and trust myself enough to get where I wanted to be."

I knew I wasn't strong enough to stay at JCSU after Brittney died. I needed to be closer to my family. Giving up on earning a degree was not an option. I wanted more for myself and the best way to honor Brittney was to make the most of my life, live out my dreams and accomplish everything I could accomplish while I had the chance. To continue, even though my soul was broken, I transferred to Claflin University in my home state of South Carolina. The emptiness and pain of depression and abuse only got bigger when I lost my cousin. She was one of the few people who cared enough to reach out to me every day. I knew I would never be as important to another person as I had been to her, and this was painfully clear as I started my second semester of college at Claflin University. Although I was closer to home, attending the college right next door to my brother's and at the same college as my best friend, Katrina; I was still very much invisible. There were many days I found myself locked in the room, trying to force myself to sleep so I would not have to be around people. I attended only a few events on campus with Katrina or my other friend Stacia. I watched the other college students interact with one another and form bonds, but I didn't understand how they could be so trusting of each other after such a short time. I wanted to develop the same intimate friendships my peers were, but I was afraid to disappoint them, afraid of their judgment and afraid of not meeting their expectations. It became clear that it wasn't that I didn't fit in, it was that I didn't know and trust myself enough to get where I wanted to be.

    I knew I wanted to be successful and education was how I would get there; however, I still didn't I believe I would ever allow myself to let go of my fear and be successful. Success depends more on who you know rather than what you know. I lacked the confidence to network and form relationships with new people; therefore, the limits I placed on myself held me back from the life I was working hard for.

    The sun was bright and the air was crisp, the coolness of the breeze caressed my warm cheeks just enough to keep me from sweating in my nervous state. As I bounced my way toward my first business class, there was slight upturn playing along with the sides of my lips and my eyes took in everything around me. The undercurrent of excitement flowed through me and pushed me one step closer to realizing my long-term goal of owning my own business. I arrived at class 5 minutes early just as I always did, but this was the first day of classes within my major. I watched as the austere party-poopers, dressed in their full business suits while holding leather, business portfolios sauntered in on the soles of their expensive loafers or pumped-up pumps. Not a hair out of place and makeup was on point as well. A few of the guys wore bow ties and others wore straight ties, their trousers were just high enough to see their socks. *I think I chose the wrong major.* The thought soaked my mind like my great aunt's lemon glaze as she pours it over her perfect-fresh-from-the-oven pound cake. They all look like they belong on Wall Street and there I was in a pair of jeans and a button up shirt, hair pulled back in a low ponytail and no makeup. *I missed the memo*!

Once class started, the professor got up and asked everyone to stand and introduce themselves. In my head, I was already prepared to give my usual, my-name-is-Juquietta-McFadden-I'm-from-South- Carolina-and-I-one-day-want-to-own-my-own-business speech, but my confidence in my words quickly dissolved when the other students stood up and presented themselves as if they were interviewing for an internship. They all knew exactly what companies they wanted to work for after graduation. The history of the companies and all. *Oh, my goodness, I am way out of my league. The history of the companies...really?* I thought about ways to escape my introduction to avoid embarrassing myself. It was too late. All the moisture from my mouth pooled into my hands and was replaced with cotton and sawdust. I couldn't fake a bathroom trip because I was next. I went with what I had already prepared because it was easier than making something up or saying nothing at all. I could feel their judgmental eyes burning through my pink button-up and all I wanted to do was get through my introduction and sit down.

Others in the school of business seemed to exude so much confidence and had amazing communication skills. Everyone seemed to make friends and connect so easily with others. As the semester continued, I kept to myself or stayed close to my friend Stacia, who was also a business major. My grades were great but I often found myself playing the comparison game to other high achieving students and I always seemed to come up lacking. Out of fear not competing with my peers, I spent very little time outside of classes on campus getting to know them. I was completely intimidated by classmates who never knew me and whom I never knew. I wonder if they had the same fears as me and if I let my fears keep me from making connections and friendships during my years at Claflin?

I needed an escape. I needed to figure out where I belonged. I needed to give myself the opportunity to be successful and make my parents proud.

My decision to join the military was mine alone, but having family members in the military did play a role in my decision to do so. The fact that my boyfriend would be enlisting added to my desire to join, too.

I ran into Travis and a few of his friend during the street dance portion of the Clarendon County's annual Striped Bass Festival on a Saturday afternoon. I had just transferred closer to Claflin and was still dealing with the death of my best friend, Brittney; but I wanted to get out and do something to take my mind off things. It was weird how Travis and I reconnected because we had originally met and played together when we were little kids during the summers I spent at my grandmother's house. Although; we often crossed paths throughout the years and always had friendly conversations, it was my third time running into him since I transferred closer to home and there was something different about running into him this time.

"Hey, how have you been? I haven't seen you in forever, what you got going on? I always ask your cousin about you." His smooth voice was hot chocolate on a cold, winter day and he had just wrapped me up in one of those teddy bear hugs he was known for giving.

"I've been good... just busy with school stuff," I said. Pretending not to notice how great his hug felt.

"Yea I know how that is, same with me. Well...it was good seeing you." He said looking me in the eyes while I avoided his like the plague.

"Good seeing you too." I walked away still thinking about the hug he had just given me. *I could fall asleep in his arms.*

"Hey!" He yelled. "Is it okay if I call you tonight?" I nodded yes and kept walking. *He won't be playing on my phone tonight, 'cause he doesn't have my number and I'm not going to give it to him either.*

***

I was not looking to be in a relationship or anything close to it. I was going to take this time in my life to just be single and focus on my goals. When God was ready for me to be in a relationship with someone again, He would make that undeniably clear to me. Lying in bed that night I got a call from an unknown number. It wasn't normal for me to answer unknown calls, but without giving a second thought I picked up the phone.

"Hello"

"Hey this is Travis"

How in the world did he get my number? "Oh hey, how did you get my number?"

"Your cousin gave it to me, I told you I was going to call you."

You wait until I see her, who told her to give out my number. "Oh, she did, she didn't tell me that she did."

"Is that a problem?

"No, it's not. I just wasn't expecting you to really call that's all."

I decided to engage in the conversation for a little while. To my surprise, I didn't want to get off the phone when it was time to hang up. I'll have to remember to thank my cousin when I talk to her again. He was very respectful and our conversations were always interesting and never went in the direction of anything sexual. We talked for weeks and one night he decided to profess his feelings and his desire to pursue a relationship with me. He respectfully asked me to be his girlfriend and explained how he would treat me. Although he was very sweet, I respectfully declined and explained to him why I was not ready for another relationship. He did not let that discourage him. We continued to talk every night for about a month. A few nights out of the week he would remind me of his offer by telling me to let him know when I was ready to accept him as my boyfriend. I loved the fact that he was so patient with me, that I could talk to him for hours about anything, that he was always respectful and sweet, and that I felt no pressure.

It started to become clear to me that God was showing me all the signs letting me know He had sent me my man, my heart still did not feel ready, so I continued to decline to be in a relationship with him. Then one night, just like most nights, we had spent hours on the phone talking. It was getting late and I knew I needed to be asleep because I had an early 8 a.m. class the next morning. Before we had the chance to tell each other good night our call was disconnected. Being it was already late and I had to be up early, I had no plans of answering the phone when he called back. I would just talk to him the next day and explain to him why I did not answer. He clearly had other plans. My phone rang back to back continuously. When will he get the hint that I am not going to pick up? *He can keep calling all he wants too but I'm going to sleep.*

When the calls continued, I started to think this guy must be crazy or possessive to be calling this many time. After the 20th call, I realized he was not going to stop until I answered the phone so I picked up. In a way, I expected him to question me about why I was not answering his calls or be upset I was ignoring him, but it was the opposite. "Hey, I apologize for calling so much I just wanted to say good night and make sure you knew I didn't hang the phone up on you on purpose." He was so sweet and it made me regret not answering the first call. When we hung up I could not sleep. God was revealing to me all of Travis' amazing qualities, the very ones I had asked for. He proved himself to be kind, smart, respectful, humble attitude, a ready smile and of course, he was Gorgeous! *Why are you not giving him a chance Quietta?*

I looked back at my phone amazed someone cared enough to call over 20 times...twenty times, just to tell me good night. His persistence and patience were the two main reasons why I knew he deserved a chance. During our conversation the next day, I knew he would ask so I waited on him to ask me to let him know when I was ready to give him a chance.

"Have you thought about my question anymore?"

"Yes."

"Okay, I'll wait as long as you want me to. Just let me know when you are ready. I want to be more than just your friend."

"I'm ready."

"Huh...what did you just say?" I could hear the excitement in his voice and it made me smile.

"I said I'm ready to give it a chance."

"You sure? You just don't know how happy I am right now." He had been asking me to be his lady for so long he and I know he didn't expect me to say yes when I did. His joy gave me more joy than I ever thought possible.

Travis joined the military a year before I joined, which was only a month after we decided that we wanted to be in a relationship. We knew the time and distance would be a test of our relationship and what we were willing to endure it to be together. Every day apart, every letter sent, and every phone call shared; made us want to be together even more. I guess the saying is true...absence makes the heart grow fonder.

After attending college for a full year, I talked to Travis about the idea of me joining the military. He was supportive of whatever I wanted to do. He went with me to talk to recruiters and each step after that. I felt content in my decision and I knew If there was anything to make my father proud, it would be me following in his footsteps and joining the military. Although our relationship was still strained; I always longed to be daddy's little girl just like before I found out daddies made mistakes and broke hearts. Just as I hoped and prayed my father was all for it!

All of my family and friends were proud to hear of my decision to join the service while still completing my college degree. All the support I was getting motivated me to continue on my journey of creating a better opportunity for myself and to push past any fear I had. My family, as well as church members and friends, recognized and congratulated my achievements and commended me for being so brave and bold. Joining the army was also a personal challenge because I needed to prove to myself I was stronger, emotionally, mentally and spiritually. I needed to prove to myself I could survive and make it without depending on my family. My first time away from home was my first semester at Johnson C. Smith University and from the beginning, I wanted to go back home to be around family. I was disappointed with myself during that first couple of months because I realized I wasn't ready to be on my own. When later in the same semester, my cousin died, I had a valid reason to pack up and come home…it made it easier, but I let myself down when I came home and I needed to prove I could make it on my own.

    I joined the army in the summer of 2010 and it felt like it was the right thing to do. I got the opportunity to travel to places I probably would never have thought about going before I became a soldier. Military life was a completely different lifestyle, but I adapted. The bond I developed with the other soldiers is one that will last a lifetime. I missed my family and friends but because we stayed busy most of the time, there was not much time to get overly emotional about not being close to them. One of my favorite things about being in Oklahoma was the beautifully colored skies and doing morning PT under the night skies where I often saw shooting stars. It was like something out of a Hallmark movie. I buried myself in my bible on Sundays after I attended church on the army base at Fort Sill Oklahoma. Reading God's word was therapeutic for me. The only communication with the outside world we were allowed was through written letters and a few minutes to use the phone every week. I received many letters from my mother and Travis; as well as a few other people from home while I was in basic training. The letters kept me updated about what was happening back home. Those letters also reminded me that someone cared. Although I gained a new family in the army, it was still important to me I was not forgotten by my family back home.

The army was different from civilian life but it helped me to grow in many ways. The challenges I faced during training made me question myself and my decisions, but with prayer, determination and the support of my platoon I made it out. The most amazing part about being in my experience was belonging to a military family who would support me no matter what I went through; I was finally important to a group of people who recognized and appreciated what I brought to the table. In the days leading to graduation from basic combat training, I was ecstatic because my family was coming to my graduation. Just like all of the other soldiers, I missed my family and I could not wait to see them.

As graduation day neared, I noticed soldiers purchasing tickets to fly home and others had family members flying in for the big event. There was no doubt in my heart my family would be there. We talked about it weeks before, but no one in my family had a ticket to fly out to see me. They ensured me they would be there. I figured even if they didn't have the tickets to fly, they would drive; the same as they had done when my brother graduated from the military. On the day, we were allowed to call home, which was only 5 days before graduation, my conversation with my mom confirmed what my gut had been telling me for weeks.

"Hello, Hey... Ma?" I let her name linger as a question between us because I knew something was off.

"Hey." She paused and didn't say anything else. I heard the truth in her silence and my heart broke.

"Mom, are you guys on the road. I graduate in a few days. I need you all to be here..." I heard her take a deep breath and blow it like she was smoking a cigarette. I knew then they were not coming and no excuse was good enough.

"We're not gonna make to your graduation. We looked online for the tickets but they are just too expensive for all of us. Your daddy did mention driving, but the way it's looking we ain't going to make it. We'll try to get to the next one, okay--"

I broke into her words, needing to say something to get them here. "Ma, please I will help with the tickets if I have to. One person can come if everybody can't just Please don't make me do this by myself...I did it and I want y'all—" She interrupts me with a gruff response.

"Quietta ain't nothing I can do, we don't have the money like that. We'll see you when you come home in a few days. I have to go. Talk with you later. So proud of you." Click...nothing. My family disappointed me, again and I almost expected it but hoped I was wrong.

As disappointed as I was, I was proud of myself because I stepped completely out of my comfort zone for once in my life and I made it through nine weeks of physical and emotional hardship. Although I was extremely proud of myself, I needed my family to be just as proud of me. I needed them to see how much I've grown and to celebrate with me.

Soldiers had what was called Family Day the day before graduation; this day was designed to let soldiers reconnect with their families before graduation and AIT. We did a special drill and ceremony performance for the families to showcase what we learned while in basic training.

There was one drill sergeant that had a smooth singing voice and when he led cadences, it gave us a sense of motivation and pride to sing along with him. He led us, singing to the field where families were waiting to greet their graduating soldiers and start Family day, Back Home Back Home

Back home where I belong
And it won't be long
til I get on back home.

I stood and scanned the crowded auditorium, looking and hoping my family would not let me celebrate this special day alone. Every shade of skin seemed to be on display; from chalk white to ebony black and every shade in between. Yet, there was not one person in the bleachers whom I could call family. The noise was deafening. "Rosa!" A woman with a heavy NY accent called out over the crowd. "Raymond! Hey, Ray...we proud uh you, man!" I saw a tall, dark and handsome man with his hands cupped around his mouth and a proud glint in his eyes. His eyes were shining with pride and my eyes were shining with unshed tears.

Once our performance ended we marched back to our barracks and waited to be released to our families. I still held out hope that someone was waiting for me. The moment we were released, soldiers and family members ran to embrace each other. There was so much love floating through the air. I could have gotten high from it if I allowed myself to sink into it. I don't ever recall seeing so many grown men shed tears as they held their sons and/or daughters. Girlfriends and boyfriends kissed and held on to each other because they knew this reunion would be over soon and AIT would take their loved ones away, again.

In a crowded room, people are hugging me, slapping me on my back and yelling congratulations; while I stand there with a plastic smile on my face and tears of hurt and insecurity trickling down my brown cheeks, I was still alone. These people have no idea what it means to be alone. *Look at all of you…laughing and whooping it up…where the heck is my family? Why am I not important enough to drive or fly for?*

"Thanks. You, too." I mechanically replied to another girl whose name I can't remember, as she passed by wrapped in her daddy's arm while he places a soft kiss on the top of her head. *I hate her!*
I was angry! I was hurt! Most of all, I was confused and left with what felt like millions of questions pounding against my skull. I fought to gain control of the depression, insecurities, and low self-esteem over the course of basic training, but it was as if all of the work I'd done came undone as I watched everyone with their families. The pain in my heart

outweighed the muscles in my face, the muscles I used to put on my fake smile. Anger and grief overpowered my thoughts and I broke down in tears while standing in the center of everyone else's joy. If they really loved me, how could they hurt me and abandon me as if I was worth nothing to any of them? I was depleted, invisible, lonely, and unworthy. Fortunately; there was a battle buddy, a partner assigned to a soldier to help assist them in and out of combat, whose family saw my hurt and tried their best to comfort me. They were a very nice white family and they insisted I join them for the rest of the day. I was grateful their kindness towards me and I enjoyed my time with them as we visited a local animal farm and ate at a historical restaurant. Her grandparent, who raised her, shared stories of their past visits to Oklahoma as well as personal stories about how they met and fell in love. My mind continuously bounced back to my own family and their obvious neglect.

    I called home, hoping to rid myself of the loneliness sitting around my neck like a noose, but instead, the phone call just tightened it further. They were all together and all I could hear was laughter in the background. They were enjoying each other while I was miles away...heartbroken because no one showed up for me. In fact, they barely spoke to me because they were talking to each other.

"Hello!" It was bad enough they were not here for me, but now I also had to yell to remind them I was on the phone.

"Hey, what you doing?" My mother asked through laughter. I could tell that she didn't really care to know and it only agitated me more when I tried to answer her question and she just talked and laughed at what was going on in the background.

"I'll just call back later". I said after a few times of shouting hello and having to repeat myself over all the noise.

"Okay," she said still laughing and not even noticing the irritation in my voice. I didn't find anything funny at all. I wanted their misery to match my own, their sadness to rival my own...in short, I wanted to know I was not suffering alone. I suddenly wished I had not gotten a plane ticket to go home for Christmas break. I was tired of feeling like I had no place in my own family. The thought of just never returning home was becoming more and more appealing.

December 9, 2010, was my official graduation from basic combat training. It was bittersweet: sweet because I accomplished so much. I found the strength within myself to cope with being alone. I was much more confident in my abilities physically and mentally and was ready to leave for my next location. Bitter because I wanted to share those moments with people who knew and loved me.

I boarded the plane to Ft. Leonardwood Missouri, where I was stationed for AIT. My military job was 88M (Motor Vehicle Operator). learned to operate and manage different types of military vehicles. I found that AIT was not as hard as basic training and by this time, I was used to being away from home and a few of my closest battle buddies from basic training and I became really close friends, too. February 11, 2011, I graduated from AIT training. Once again no one showed up. My accomplishments suddenly felt insignificant. I realized my decision to join the Army Reserves wasn't my decision at all. I joined hoping my family and friends would finally see me as a strong and capable person who could make it on my own

My desire to be in the military changed shortly after I got back home. When I reported to my station once a month for duty I would fall into depression and began to have anxiety attacks. The attacks came anytime I saw a group of soldiers in uniform. Weekend drills became unbearable for me. I remember the first time it happened. I sat stiff as a board surrounded by soldiers wearing the same uniform as me. Visions of combat attacks clouded my thoughts. My heart beat double time. My palms got sweaty before the heat radiated to the rest of my body. I couldn't breathe, it felt as if I swallowed a golf ball; my airways blocked. I ran to the nearest bathroom, panting and frightened at what was happening to me. It was the first time that the sight of soldiers, just like myself, made me feel like I was going to die. The last formation was only a few minutes away. I stayed in the bathroom until It was time for formation. I was too scared to look at anyone during formation so I tried my best to look past them. Before formation ended, I could feel my body changing again as if another attack was going to happen. I rushed out the door to my car and sat there with my eyes closed repeating to myself everything was going to be okay, but nothing was okay. The attacks started with just seeing others in uniform, then they came at just the thought of being in the army. Each attack got progressively worse. I knew I had to finally do something to save my mental health when I started to have thoughts of suicide, just to get out. Getting into the military was not hard, but when it came down to needing to get out...the struggle got real.

    The anxiety and the depression made me feel like I was literally losing my mind. I knew getting out was not going to be easy but I knew for my own health I had too. Things got worse every month. My mind was telling me there was only one way out and that one way... was death. I shared with Travis what I was going through. He was very concerned, as I expected him to be, he ensured me he would support me if I decided to get out of the military. He saw me through my anxiety and did his best to comfort me through the depression. I was afraid if anyone knew about my attacks I would be judged.   Once again depression had taken over and was becoming too much for me to handle. The change began to show in my attitude, my body language, my conversations and everything else. My father was the first to notice the change in me; I was living like I had no purpose, just waiting for my time to come. Not knowing what day, it was or what to even do with me. To get me help, my father set up a session for me to speak with my pastor. I opened to my pastor about what I was going through and the voices I heard in my head telling me I had to kill myself to get out. He informed me there was always another way, even in the military. He advised me to communicate with my chain of command and find out how to first reach the Chaplain. I built a relationship with the Chaplain who referred me to a counselor and they both were true live savers.

    Once again, I found myself sitting in front of complete strangers trying to understand life. My entire chain of command was supportive and wanted what was best for me. I hated my time in the army ended as soon as it did, but I was relieved I had not lost my mind. I made the decision to join the army seeking the approval of others and hoped the benefits would help me become successful; that decision caused me to lose my mind and almost my life. This experience taught me I could not live my life to please everyone else. I judged for my decision to get out the military; some people joked that I faked mental illness to receive benefits and others speculated I just couldn't handle the heat so I cried my way out. Truthfully the jokes were disturbing. It led me to understand not everyone will feel what I feel. No matter how much I tried to explain and elaborate on my experiences with mental illness, no one else could ever understand my hurt because they're not experiencing it.

    Many people do not understand mental illness. People who do deal with some kind of mental illness are often afraid to reach out to anyone out of fear of being judged, made fun of or dismissed as crazy. African American women are expected to be strong and raised to pray through it; however, the reality is when dealing with mental issues...your thoughts are hijacked and you're no longer in control of how you think, feel and/or respond to those feelings and thoughts. It was a season that came and went quickly, but this short season in my life gave me strength and confidence I would never have had, had not I gone through it.

~prayer~

Dear God

I went out into the world trying to figure life out on my own. Many days I felt lost and alone not knowing who I had to depend on when even family disappointed. Following my own plans and the plans of others led me down a few dead-ends and left me struggling to find my way back. I now know all along all I had to do was follow you. Wherever you lead I will follow and wherever you send me I will go because I know that you are there.

_____

_____

_____

_____

_____

_____

_____

_____

Chapter 5

Our unconditional love and support for one another gave us both what we needed to grow together as well as individually.

My civilian life was not what I thought it would be when I petitioned and earned my discharge from the military. My plans were to go to finish college, meet new friends, have amazing new experiences, find a great job and create the life I always dreamed of. Instead, the test of life came and I got a major reality check. Once again, I hated my life and wondered why God created me.

All was not bad. The relationship that Travis and I built was growing stronger with each passing day. We laughed, cried, prayed and worshipped together and we helped each other to reach our goals. He remained the same sweet, hardworking guy I met at Striped Bass Street Festival two years ago. There were days I questioned if I was doing the right thing by being in a relationship with him, but he gave me no reason to go back on my decision. I supported and stuck by him while he was away at military training and helped him to continue college when he returned. He gave me the same support I gave him and motivated me to stay focused no matter how hard things got.

There was something different about him compared to other guys. The more time we spent building our relationship, the more God revealed to me he wasn't just a temporary boyfriend. His calm, humble spirit pulled me in and wrapped around my heart like a nice warm blanket. My body felt light, the heaviness of pain I carried for so long was now replaced with peace. I didn't deserve him, at least that's what I told myself because I was spiritually broken after dealing with insecurity, neglect, and depression prior to meeting him. I knew what we were building was a game changer for both of us and I was determined to keep it healthy and whole, even as I faced my own personal demons. I didn't want to make him responsible for all the hurt and fear from my past relationships, but most of me didn't know how to maintain a healthy relationship with him and continue to deal with the pain and insecurities plaguing me from past hurts. Like any woman who has ever been hurt or disappointed in previous relationships, with each heartbreak and disappointment the stones built one on top of the other and built a wall around my heart, to guard it against being hurt again. A wall he was not afraid to tear down to claim his rightful position not in my heart, but in my infinite soul. Because that's where our love for one another resides...in our souls.

He wasn't intimidated by my efforts to keep him from getting too close. His love for me was stronger than the stones in my heart, so little by little the bricks came crumbling down but my heart was still intact. I was afraid of letting him in; afraid he would see my flaws or think I had too much baggage in my life to continue to be with me. He proved to me through his words and his actions there was nothing he wasn't willing to go through with me. Instead of taking the easy road and pushing me away when he learned about my past, he pulled me closer and assured me he still thought I was nothing short of amazing and beautiful. I never felt comfortable opening up to anyone about my past until I was with him. There was never a time I felt weak with him. He helped me recognize the strength I carried within myself; a strength I never even knew I had. Not only was he a blessing to me, but that *I could* be the same for him felt amazing. To know someone knew all my flaws and still loved me unconditionally and still saw only the best in me; I finally understood how God loves me...how He sees me as fearfully and wonderfully made.

I won't say he completed me and vice-versa, but we certainly did enhance each other. Our unconditional love and support for one another gave us both what we needed to grow together as well as individually. His strengths became my strengths and mine were his. We shared not only our love, support, and truth but the very strength of our souls...there was only one way our relationship could go...

I graduated with my Bachelor's of business management, three years after meeting and falling in love with Travis. Shortly before I graduated, we found out we were expecting our first child. I was having a child with the man I hoped to spend the rest of life with. I received two job offers a couple of months after graduating. As difficult as my life was before I met and fell in love with Travis, living became just as easy after falling in love with him. Our relationship created a soul tie which made me stronger and more secure. Through our love for God and each other, we were gifted with more than we ever thought possible. Life was exciting and a little overwhelming, but it was all coming together. A year after graduating, landing my first job and moving into my first home, and six months after discovering we were expecting; Travis asked me to marry him...and unlike the times he asked me to be his girlfriend, I did not make him wait and repeat the question 50-11 times before giving him a yes. It was immediate and sure!

***

I was exhausted from working a full 40 hours at work that week, but being 8 months pregnant and getting a whiff of the smell of bacon was enough to wake me up.

"Good morning babe," Travis said walking into our bedroom with a full plate of grits, eggs, bacon, sausage, and toast, my favorite.

"Good morning, is that for me?"

"Yes, it is." He replied while passing me the plate of food. It was not unusual for him to bring me breakfast in bed. It was something I became accustomed to him doing.

"What do you think about riding down to the beach today, just the two of us." He asked.

"That would be fun, it's a beautiful Saturday we might as well enjoy it."

"Okay finish your food and get dressed."

On the ride to the beach, we made a few stops; the first was to get something comfortable for me to wear. I picked out a light blue sundress and some flip flops.

"Where do you want to go first?"

"It would be relaxing to sit by the ocean and enjoy the breeze for a while." At the beach, we wet our feet a little and found a comfortable spot to relax and talk. Travis just couldn't sit still. He found a group of guys throwing a football in the ocean and joined them. I wondered where his courage to go as far in the ocean as he did came from. Any other time we went to the beach, he expressed how he would never be caught going so far out. We went for ice cream at the same parlor we went to on our very first beach trip together. Later we visited Broadway at the Beach. We shopped and ate and caught a movie.

"Are you happy, baby?" He asked.

"Yes," I replied.

"I'm going to make you the happiest girl in the world before tonight ends." He said while kissing me on the cheek. *I already am* I thought to myself. We walked around enjoying the live bands and the scenery. He kept reminding me how he loved me. None of his actions were out of the ordinary. He was always affectionate and expressive with his feelings. My feet started to swell after walking around on them for so long and I suggested we head home.

"Did you enjoy your day baby? I just wanted to show you how much I love you and enjoy a fun day before the baby comes, but I have something for you…close your eyes." I suspected for a second he might be proposing but he could also just be giving me another just-because-gift. I heard him fumbling with something for a few minutes.

"You can open your eyes now." I opened my eyes to see him facing me with a tiny little box that held a gorgeous silver engagement ring set.

"Will you Marry me?" My mouth fell open and my eyes stretched wide. Whatever he said in that moment fell on deaf ears. Somebody needed to pinch me because this had to be a dream. After 4 years of dating and wondering how and when this moment would happen, I was finally standing in it. I looked from the ring to his handsome brown face.

"Are you serious?" I squealed. "Travis don't be playing like that, are you serious?"

"I'm serious baby, this is for real, will you marry me?"

"Well, Duh!?" I said wrapping my arms around him. I buried my face in his chest, trembling from the excitement, "Oh My God, Oh my God, Oh my God." I repeated each time in a different tone.

"I told you I was going to make you the happiest girl in the world before tonight was over." His Cheshire cat grin split his entire face in two...I'm sure it mirrored my own.

"I love you so much." I whisper-cried through the tears now running down my face.

"I love you more." He said pulling me in for another kiss. We basked in the moment and celebrated with dinner at Olive Garden before calling our families. Exactly one month after getting engaged, I gave birth to our first child; a beautiful, healthy baby girl who we named Talayna. I never knew my heart could hold so much love, but apparently, the heart has a much greater capacity to grow with love than I ever imagined.

The following year, August 9 we were married *officially* before God and all of our family and friends. Our souls were connected and our hearts were already one, the marriage was just the celebration of our union. A few weeks before our wedding, we received the surprise of our lives when we found out we were expecting our second baby! My heart was so full! My excitement level was through the roof.

I snatched the phone off the counter "It's positive" I screamed to my fiancee. His reply was

" I already knew."

I recognized we were blessed but there was also a part of me that was scared to death because my life was changing so dramatically! The life I dreamed about was becoming my reality and I barely had time to even appreciate it as it happened. Although the changes were good and positive, I knew I was still battling my own demons and fear warred with joy and made for a volatile mix of self-doubt. *I wish I would have sought God's guidance on the new responsibilities with which He entrusted me. I wish I knew how to love myself first so I could love my husband and kids the way they deserved to be loved. I wish I was more stable mentally and financially.*

I imagined I would have my degree, get a good job, marry the man of my dreams and become a mother. However; I never imagined it would all happen in a matter of two years. My arms and heart were open to God and He continued to bless me with love, support, joy, and growth. I was constantly reminded of God's promise to be faithful to those who love Him. Despite how I ever felt about myself, God still saw me as worthy to be the helpmate of a great man, and the mother and steward of not one, but two of His precious souls.

My husband and two daughters are constant reminders of God's love for me. For every time I looked in the mirror and hated who and what stared back at me; I now look at the beautiful angel-faced babies and know that a part of their beauty comes from me. For every time, I felt like I was unworthy of love; I am reminded that out of all the women in the world, my husband chose me. For every time, I couldn't see myself beyond the negative self-image I embraced as truth; I am reminded of all the prodigious accomplishments and how far I have come.

It felt even better to know without a doubt this was a love brought together by God. Being in a relationship was the last thing on my mind when Travis came into my life. I was broken and not trying to add another worrisome situation to my life. Relationships can be stressful and I was already dealing with enough. I learned if it is God's will for us to be together then nothing and no one can change it. The person God sent did not come in the package that normally caught my eye, but nothing else worked with anyone else who did because it wasn't God's will. It all began to make sense to me. All the times Travis and I ran into each other there was always a reason for us to just go on about our lives, but even I couldn't deny with every encounter there was a feeling that passed over me. I didn't get *that* feeling when talking to any other guy. God knew when it was time and He knew what both our hearts needed.

I grew up playing tag with Travis, I never thought he would mean so much to me or thought he would be the one to help me through so many issues or more importantly, that he would someday be my husband and the father of my children. God has his own way of working things out.

I like to think He already has each of our lives planned for us already. Everything goes according to his plans and not our plans for ourselves. I've come to realize His plans are far better than any I could have come up with on my own. Many women spend their lives searching for a man to love them the way my man loves me. When I focused on myself and my relationship with God, He sent just who and what He had for me when the time was right. The last thing I wanted was for the right person to come at the wrong time or for the wrong person to come at the right time. Both of those situations could cause a lifetime of unnecessary heartache, pain, stress, and drama.

God already knew what I wanted and needed. He didn't need me to continue to pray for him to send me a good man, with lots of money, no baby mamas, tall, dark and handsome. God wanted to see me working and praying to better myself first. When he sent my husband, he wanted to know I could help him on his journey through life, through his brokenness, and his struggles and not just look for him to be fine, pay my bills, and spoil me. *My life was not meant to be a Destiny's Child song.* I often say God sent my soulmate earlier than I expected simply because it was the right time. When I think about the what-ifs, the truth is if we were together sooner we would not have lasted and if it had been later then we would not have been able to help each other through some of the most important times in our lives. The lesson in it was letting God take charge and trusting His plans for my life. God sent Travis to shine a light on the beauty in me that I could never see.

~prayer~

Dear God

Your love is unconditional and everlasting, but still, you saw fit to bless me with even more. You saw me worthy to be a wife and a mother, even when I felt so undeserving of your blessings. Father help me to be a representation of your love for them. I thank you for the gift of life and love. Help me to be as much of a blessing to them as they are to me. Amen

Chapter 6

"Our desire was to safeguard the girls from the pain, anxiety, and hopelessness we were feeling."

My husband and I had a beautiful wedding! I arrived at the church with my best friend, Katrina, and my cousin, Niesha, who was my maid and matron of honor.

"Are you nervous?" Niesha asked.

"No, I'm just ready to see him," I said, wondering how Travis was feeling and what he looked like.

"Awe... my best friend is getting married." Katrina teased.

The two of them reflected on when Travis and I first started dating over 5 years ago, pointing out that I was the happiest they ever saw me and how they always knew he would be the one I would marry. We entered the church through the back door, still reflecting on my happiness and hoping no one would see us. We were greeted by my bridesmaids, they were already dressed and looking beautiful as garden flowers in their satin knee length turquoise dresses, and red heels.

"Oh my God y'all look so beautiful," I said as gratitude and love spilled down my cheeks. I walked over to, Keyana, who was holding my one-year-old daughter, Talayna who wore a gorgeous white dress decorated with turquoise petals; the white halo around her head was the perfect touch for our angel. "Look at my baby!" I smiled. This wedding was more than a celebration of how through our love for each other and God's love for us, two beautiful lives were created.

We were raised in the south and having two kids before we were married did not go over well with some of my family. I was told Travis would never marry me and I would end up a single mother raising two kids alone. The overwhelming feeling of completion expanded and filled the space which had previously been a gaping hole of self-doubt and fear. I thought about how once I didn't believe I deserved to be loved by anyone, how I almost believed my kid's and I would become another statistic. The reality was, Travis *really* loved us and leaving us was just not in his character. August 9, 2014, was all about *our* little family. I remembered the scripture I spoke over our relationship from the very beginning; Mark 10:9, "Therefore what God has joined together let no one separate." I used my hands to fan away the tears.

"Okay, let me go get dressed I don't want to cry just yet." I laughed. Katrina and Niesha helped me into my beaded lace gown, the material a whisper against my skin, while I got my makeup and hair done.

So much was going on around me, but my mind was on my soon-to-be husband who I knew was somewhere in the church preparing to take our vows. I wasn't nervous at all, just ready to become Mrs. Travis Witherspoon. I could hear the music he and his best men were to enter too. *It's starting.* Chill Bumps covered my skin. I heard my aunt Mary Jane getting my bridesmaids and flower girls lined up to walk in.

"Alright girls, you know where you belong, shortest to tallest and I need my flower girls over here." When their music began to play my aunt peeked back in the private room I was in. "You ready?" She asked giving me a smile.

"I'm ready." I smiled. I said a quick prayer to myself, positioned my bouquet of red and turquoise flowers in front of me and gracefully walked out of the room. My dad was there waiting; although he didn't say much... the way his eyes welled up and his double-take and frozen posture when he saw me standing there in my white A-line gown, decorated with tiny pearls and a turquoise sash that flowed behind me along with the train, told me he was seeing me as a woman and not a little girl anymore. I could see Travis's silhouette standing underneath the beautifully decorated arch through the stained glass of the french-doors. When the doors opened I could see the guests standing out of the corner of my eye, but my focus was on the handsome man standing there in his gray suit, white shirt and vest, and a necktie and handkerchief that matched the sash on my dress. I walked along the white runner floating past the trail of red petals the flower girls left. The pews were draped with crisp white linen with just the right amount of flowers. Our eyes connected, much like our souls and the river of joy flowed from him to me and back to him again… it was everything. There were few if any dry eyes in the building as we professed our love to and for one another through our vow.

   Our wedding was all we dreamed it would be. We soaked in each moment of our day. The excitement was like electricity sliding along the surface of our skin. The joy was champagne bubbles tickling our noses. We were ensconced in the simplicity of being newlyweds!

   Months before our wedding, we decided to move into a nicer, more expensive apartment before finding out we were expecting our second child. We moved into our new home one week after our wedding in August. We were still on cloud nine from being newlyweds and having the plans we made for our lives come together, but we realized with all the major life-changes in our lives which brought much excitement; there were even more responsibilities.

God continued to show us a favor in all endeavors, but we were not prepared to be good stewards of all we were favored with. He was gracious enough to give us the desires of our hearts, but instead of us seeking guidance and waiting for him to direct our paths, we made decisions on our own and those self-directed decisions set us back. All that we had amassed, we were destined to have. It may not; however, have been the right time, but our road in life was already mapped out for us and that road would lead us to our destiny. Sometimes we move ahead of God and instead of following the path He has set us on, we wander for forty years in the wilderness when we were only forty days from our destiny. Regardless of what road we took, our destination did not change; however, the path that started so easily did change and we had to take responsibility for our choices and accept the consequences of our actions.

The nicer apartment we moved into came with a higher rent and as reality settled around us like a heavy, wet blanket, we realized the income that had been enough before was not going to cut it anymore. Considering we now had to provide for ourselves, a toddler and a newborn in roughly 7 months, we knew we had to make some changes. As my belly continued to expand with our miracle, my soul became more diseased with the mounting bills, responsibilities, and fear of not being able to make it all work out. I know both my husband and I were doing all we could do to make the best life for our family, but our best never seemed to be enough. The truth was, it wasn't enough and we knew it wasn't...but we continued to work toward making it work.

Money or the lack of money was a constant headache. My husband and I argued about small, unimportant things that never bothered us before. I wish I could say it was pregnancy hormones, but it wasn't. It was stress and it was creating tension in our home.

Conversations became all about the bills and when and how they were due. Time was winding down, each month that passed meant another month closer to giving birth to our second child and there we were each month still trying to figure out how we were even going to afford to pay the rent and keep the lights on; let alone afford the added expenses of a newborn. I felt like a failure. *How could I be bringing another child into this chaos?* After an eternity of trying to wade through the ocean of stress that pushed my husband and me together only to pull us apart again, we decided it would be best for us to find a more affordable place to live to better meet the financial needs of our growing family. With only two months left before we would welcome our second daughter into the world, we found ourselves out of doors.

Although the beginning of our marriage and the birth of our second child was not going exactly as we planned; and we faced hardships during the process of securing a more affordable place to live, we were blessed to both be welcomed back to our respective parents' homes...meaning we would have to live separately until we were able to afford to get our own place.

Being newly married, having a toddler, being pregnant and not having the option to be together under the same roof was one of the most disappointing and frustrating times in my life. I felt like I was failing as a wife and as a mother. Home is where the heart is, I didn't feel at home because a part of my heart was not there with me. Not only was I hurt because my family was separated but the living situation was a lot to handle. My mother invited me back to the home I grew up in; however, I knew I was unwelcome. It was obvious by the nasty grimace my father gave me every time he walked in the house. After being there for about two weeks the arguing began.

The sun was just beginning to rise on Saturday morning, I squeezed my eyes and threw the cover my head. He had flicked on the lights and was calling my name like I was in trouble or something. Earlier in the week, he asked me to contribute to the light bill. I agreed and let him know it would be Friday before I could get it to him.

"You got that money for the bill?" Through a sleepy moan, I told him I had it but I did not have a chance to make it to the ATM yet. "What do you mean? I told you I needed the money Friday. This is all you want to do is lay around and sleep. You can't stay in here for free." I didn't say much in hopes of avoiding an argument. "Okay...I just have to go to the ATM."

"No, you didn't have any intentions of getting it. You expect to just stay up in somebody else's house for free. With a baby...and you *married*? You need to be in your own place anyway."

I was furious. I did not want to be there any more than he wanted me there. My husband and I were working diligently every day to find a home. He searched in the mornings before he went to work and he met me every day on my lunch break to search before he went to work at night.

The arguments with my father continued. I feared the arguing and stressing would cause harm to my unborn daughter. To avoid seeing and arguing with him, after work I would shower and lock myself and my daughter in the room until the next morning. *Not much of a life.* Every night after she fell asleep, I called Travis to pray, and once we hung up I cried myself to sleep. I was embarrassed that this is what my life had come to. I missed the laughter and love that filled the home my husband and I once shared. I craved the back rubs my husband gave to put me to sleep every night. I just wanted my joy back. We searched relentlessly, but for weeks it seemed we were hitting one dead end after the next.

In the Winter of 2015 before our second daughter was born, we completed paperwork for a single wide trailer home with a company that was finally agreeing to rent to us. Other companies required a higher credit score or more income and at the time, we just didn't have it. Our new home would not be ready for us to move into for approximately two weeks after the expected due date. My husband came to help around the house and spend as much time as possible with my daughter and me, but it just wasn't the *same* as being together in our own home. If we were living as a family in our own home and we didn't have the financial concerns that plagued us at every turn, we would be redecorating and creating space for the new baby and helping our toddler pick out the perfect big-sister gift for the new baby. We would spend our nights all cuddled in the bed taking turns reading to my belly and fussing over who's turn it is to pick a movie. The stress wasn't *so* bad after we knew for sure we would soon be able to have our family together in our own home again.

***

Our family was finally able to move into our new home and it was right on time because roughly two weeks later, the day after Valentine's Day, Trinity was born. I remember looking in her face thinking how much she looked like her big sister when she was born. Perfect and beautiful in her prelapsarian, innocence shown through her beautiful eyes when she looked at us. Even though I went through so much stress while carrying, her she still came out happy and healthy. Looking back on the birth of my second daughter, I understand why the Bible says we must become as little children. What she came here with is all she would ever need. We are born with everything we will ever need to be happy, healthy and whole; we need only acknowledge its existence.

The home we moved into was just a simple, white, two bedrooms, single-wide trailer in a mobile home community. The first thing I noticed was the porch and the nice sized yard. I envisioned myself sitting outside watching the kids play while my husband did yard work. The rooms were not very big but it was enough for us. It was completely different from any of our other places. It wasn't anything spectacular, but we were more than grateful to once again have a place of our own. We considered it nothing short of a blessing because we could live under the same roof, create memories together and enjoy family time. It was the first home the four of us lived in as a family. The dark clouds over our lives were moving and the sun was beginning to shine for us again. *And thank God for the sun because I don't think I could have continued much longer under all the shade my father was throwing my way.*

My husband and I were both still working our full-time jobs me as a teller and him a correctional officer. We both made over minimum wage. We enrolled the kids in a child development center only about three minutes away from my job and we found ourselves settling into a routine which created structure, joy, and happiness for all of us. For about 4 months life was stress-free; however, the added expense of childcare for two children, new furniture and the everyday household expenses associated with having a family of four started to overwhelm us...*again*.

I remember one night after putting the girls to bed, I tiptoed out of the room, went to the closet and pulled out my old purses. There was only enough milk to make one more bottle for Trinity and there were no more diapers. We didn't have any money and we had already overdrafted our accounts to pay the bills. I rummaged through the purses desperately trying to find anything I could sell and praying to come across at least a couple of dollars. I thought I heard my husband wake up so I paused until I was sure he was still asleep. I didn't want to tell him they were out of diapers and milk. I knew if he knew, he would feel obligated to call someone for money only to hear how they didn't have it. I knew every time he had to call someone for money, it hurt his pride a little bit more. I wanted to save him from feeling the guilt and shame. I sat on the floor surrounded by purses and old receipts. I came up with only enough to buy a half of gallon of whole milk. Trinity was still on formula milk but it was a sacrifice that had to be made for her to eat. I walked outside to call my brother to borrow $5.00 for a pack of diapers. My husband couldn't know. He was already beating himself up. *Sometimes being a wife, a good wife, means doing what you feel is best even if it means keeping some things to yourself to save your husband's dignity.*

Every day after work, we took turns going to family member's houses to get a good meal in the afternoons when our money wouldn't stretch. We were once again robbing Peter to pay Paul. *Whoever the heck Peter and Paul were...* Every bill we had, including rent, was paid weeks after they were due. We barely had money to take care of our responsibilities and there was no extra money to do anything else with.

My husband and I tried our best to keep one another encouraged and uplifted even as we faced financial hardships and uncertainty. We reminded each other every day it was only a test and we would get through it together.

I sat up with my back against the headboard. I glared at Travis sitting on the edge of the bed. I did not have to study his body language long to notice he was stressed. He sat with his arms propped on his knees and his head in his hands. We had just pulled a notice of eviction from the door and the lights were due to be turned off soon. I was stressing over it myself, but I knew it was harder on him being the man of the house. He was doing his best to take care of his family, we both were, but everything was falling apart. I scooted closer to him, wrapped my arms around him in a bear hug from behind. I could feel the tension in his body.

"Babe, give me your hands." I sat beside him and took his hands in mine. "Let's pray." He rolled his eyes and leaned his head back as if he had lost all faith. "I know this is hard but we are going to make it through this. We can't give up now... we have two beautiful girls depending on us." We closed our eyes and prayed.

"You're right baby, we're good, we got this." He smiled and gave me a kiss on the forehead. Honestly, I wasn't sure we would be good, but

Travis was always the stronger more positive one of the two of us. If he crumbled I would not have anyone to lift me up. *Self-preservation and all...*

Our main concern, of course, was our children. We made every sacrifice to ensure Talayna and Trinity did not vicariously experience our stress. Our desire was to safeguard the girls from the pain, anxiety, and hopelessness we were feeling. It was not easy and most of the time we felt as if we were failing them, but the horror of not working to protect them forged a determination within us to fight harder to give them the life we wanted them to have. We did not have extra money to go to the movies, the museums or even the dollar store to buy toys; therefore, the community parks became our escape. We may not have had the funds to do much but, we did not want to rob our kids of the rainbow-daydreams and ice cream covered, sticky-faced kisses of summer; so, we spent time at the parks as a family. To keep our sanity, we had to get creative. To stave off crazy, my husband and I employed creative ways to enrich our family life. Books were a staple in our home and reading stories to our girls was an easy and fun way to pass the time. My husband and I would take turns reading in this funny voice that always pulled giggles from our bellies. We were struggling but we were still together and we still had our faith.

We struggled and scraped by for months, but even as we continued to work hard it was not enough. I could not just settle for the current position I had any longer. It was not enough for my family to live comfortably. Every chance I got I applied for higher positions within the company I was working for, but nothing ever panned out. My husband and I decided it was time to take a chance and move to Charlotte where there were more opportunities. We had always talked about relocating after graduating from college but decided to stay in South Carolina because we wanted to raise our children around family while they were young.

My husband had one interview in Charlotte and was offered a job In May 2015. We didn't want to move until we both had jobs, which meant having his position held for a few months to give me time to find a job. One week after he was offered the job in Charlotte, I received the call for multiple interviews within the company I was working for. There was one position I had my heart set on. In late June, I was offered the job. Now *that* we both had job offers we could take the next steps towards making that move. However, after a financial fitness background check the company decided I was no longer qualified for the position. The disappointment crippled my motivation. I was trying and praying so hard for the position to work out. All I wanted was to help create a better life for my family. The opportunity to move and to grow in the position I desired was gone. Giving up was not an option but I must admit, I was discouraged and slightly defeated. My husband was understanding. He knew how bad I wanted this move for us. He told me not to give up and that there were so many more opportunities in Charlotte. On his days off he took time out to search other opportunities for me.

  We returned our focus on creating a more stable life for our family when we accepted the fact we would not be moving anytime soon. The struggles did not get easier for us in fact, more challenges came our way.

  The disappointment of missed opportunity settled around me like a dense fog, a new kind of despair came knocking on our door…literally. I was taking a bath to relax and clear my head when I heard a knock on our front door. Neither my husband nor I were expecting any company, so I was curious to know who was there. My husband came in the bathroom where I was.

"Babe, the furniture company is here. They have to get the stuff." His voice was calm but his face was in distress.

"What!? All of it!?" I questioned. *What else could go wrong?* Every piece of furniture in the house was on the same account. "So where are we supposed to sleep?" I was no longer relaxed.

"We'll have to figure that out, but they said they have to take everything right now." I shook my head and let out a deep sigh of frustration. "I know how you're feeling right now, it's just one thing after another but we'll figure something out." He closed the door and walked out.

I stayed in the bathroom and prayed as they disassembled and carried out the furniture we had. I prayed God would help us to remain strong and that he would make a way for us to not have our babies sleeping on the floor. The house looked different without the furniture. All that was left were our clothes and tv sitting on the floor. My husband took me by the hand and pulled me closer to him. He gave me the hug he knew I so desperately needed. He promised me things would be okay and we would not be struggling much longer.

Thankfully, just a couple of days before our furniture was taken I had purchased a toddler bed for Talayna. That night my husband and I slept on the floor, Trinity slept next to us in her car seat and Talayna slept on the mattress from her toddler bed since we hadn't gotten around to putting it together yet. I silently cried myself to sleep. I could sense my husband was feeling broken at that moment as well. *God, how did we get here? We've worked so hard to try and build a great life for our family. Everything that we had is gone. Where are we going to get money to afford new furniture? Lord. I really don't want my family to be apart again. Please help us.* My heart ached so bad thinking of how our shortcomings were now affecting our kids. The next day when we took the girls to childcare, one of the lunch ladies ran down the hall to catch me before leaving.

"Hey, baby. I was cleaning out my garage and came across a pack-n-play that we don't need and I know you got them, two girls, …it's yours if you want it." For a minute, I stood their eyes stretched, my mouth fell open, taken aback that she was offering to just give us a pack and play. *Had she known what last night was like for us?*

"Oh my God! You have no idea how much I appreciate this blessing. We can *definitely* use it. Thank you so much for thinking of my family.".

"I'll have my husband bring it up here and when you come to pick the girls up, you get it then. Have a good day, sweetie." Walking out the door I held my breath and blinked back tears. I knew it was not a coincidence she had a pack and play at just the right time. She could have asked any of the parents but instead, it was me. "Thank you, God" I repeated my gratitude repeatedly. I thanked God for answering my prayers so quickly. Our baby girl would not have to sleep another night in her car seat. As planned, when we picked the girls up that afternoon she gave us the pack and play. She had no idea how grateful we really were for her kindness. My husband and I continued to sleep on the floor for a couple of weeks, but we didn't mind much if our babies were able to sleep comfortably. We both wanted to keep our business private so we wouldn't face judgment or have our business spread around town, but we knew the only way we could get help is if we asked for it. There were a couple of family members who offered us their extra beds and couches and we humbly accepted. We had enough to be comfortable and we were thankful. We knew the value of family and faith. It was more important than material things. We continued to make our own fun at home together instead of spending money to go out somewhere.

Just as we were regaining our hope and trying to rebuild our lives, we lost our only vehicle to the 1000-year flood which came and left many in our state devastated. We rented a vehicle to get us to and from where we needed to go, but the fee was too much to continue to rent. The insurance did not cover the balance on our vehicle so we were left to still pay for the car we could no longer drive. My father offered to help us make a down payment on a new vehicle so we could have a way back and forth to work and keep our jobs. Given the history between my father and me, I was both surprised and thankful for his offer to help. He stood true to his word and helped us get a new vehicle. I realized some relationships take longer than others to heal. That one act let me know he did care. Although our relationship was not the best, he was trying to show me he had my back.

~prayer~

Dear God

I thank you for the reminder that seasons change. We go through good days and we go through some tough days but with you, we'll never have to go through them alone. Even during the storms, I still have so many reasons to praise you. You blessed me with everything I needed and took what I thought I needed to help me to realize life is about much more than the materialistic things that we own. Despite what the situation looks like I know that I am truly rich because I have you.

Chapter 6.5:

Our marriage was being tested in more ways than one and because I was already emotionally and mentally drained. I no longer had the energy or strength to fight for it.

Around the same time, my husband and I faced some issues in our marriage that practically tore us apart. My husband was always a drinker, but the stress in our lives caused him to turn to alcohol excessively. I would walk around the house and find bottles hidden in different areas of our home. I did not recognize the man I married. He was becoming a person I did not like. The more he drank the more disconnected we became. I didn't know how to deal with the change. We were barely talking at all, but I wanted my best friend back.

It was a Friday night and I was winding down from a long day of work. I hopped out of the shower and into my bed clothes. Travis was sitting in the living room with the lights off. He had his phone in his hand and earbuds in. Lately, that's all he ever did. He did not want to be around me. I suspected something was going on, but I didn't have any proof. I went to the living room to get him, to spend some quality time together since the girls were asleep and we needed to reconnect. "Babe come in the room and cuddle with me," I pratically begged.

"Okay, I'll be there in a minute, hold on.?" I could smell alcohol on his breath. "I'm coming. Go ahead."

I went to the room and found the remote to try and find a movie. Fifteen minutes passed and Travis was still in the living room. "Travis, are you coming?" I yelled.

"Yea! I said I would be there in a minute, hold on." He sounded annoyed.

After another 15 minutes, I gave up. I turned the T.V. off and turned over to go to sleep. About an hour later, I woke up. Travis must have just gotten in the bed. His phone was on the table next to me and it was still unlocked. I was curious to see what he had been doing on it so much lately. I picked up the phone gently, looking back to make sure he didn't wake up. It was on his Facebook messenger. My heart skipped a few beats. I was afraid to look but I did anyway, I wanted to know. I felt fire all through my body. My mouth was clenched so tight I could hear my teeth grit. My husband, whom I had trusted so much, had been messaging back and forth with other women. I was so betrayed. There I was begging for him to cuddle with me and he was in the other room messaging other women. Giving them the attention I was practically begging for. I screamed his name a few times to wake him up. I confronted him about the messages. He was too intoxicated to even understand what I was screaming about. I packed up the kids and spent the night at my mom's house.

Our marriage was being tested in more ways than one and because I was already emotionally and mentally drained. I no longer had the energy or strength to fight for it. My husband was my best friend and life, bad decisions and struggles were pulling us apart. He was the person that I always talked to about the highs and lows of my life and now my anchor needed anchoring, too.

I returned home the day after I found out my husband broke promises made on August 09, 2014. I needed space from him for a while so he stayed at his mother's house. The next few weeks were a roller coaster of emotions for us. He called every day, multiple times a day; but there were some days I didn't feel like hearing his voice. He knew the pain I dealt with in my life. He promised he wouldn't hurt me in *any* way. I did not feel the need to forgive him. He didn't care about my feelings, so why should I care about his. I had to seek God about what to do next. I wanted to be done, but it wasn't that easy. We made a vow before God that we would be together for better or worse. Then God reminded me that I wasn't perfect in my marriage and that I should give him the same forgiveness he gave me.

We took our time and reconnected through prayer, taking the necessary time out to do things together, and seek the professional help we needed for ourselves and for our marriage. Our marriage grew stronger, and the brief time that we were separated because of trouble, we realized that being apart was not what either of us ever wanted. Our love was stronger than any of our troubles.

Even though we were working on our relationship, my life still seemed to be falling apart and the pressure and stress started to get the best of me. One morning as I sat out to drop the girls off at school, before heading to work; all my fears, anger, and confusion I was holding in and going through started playing in my head like a horror film. I suddenly got an excruciating headache and the world around me seemed to be spinning. My heart began to beat rapidly. I was having a panic attack. I pulled over and waited until I was calm enough to dial my mother's number. I tried to speak so she could understand me, but the tears would not stop and I was struggling to catch my breath. She told me over and over to calm down and breathe so she could understand me. When I was finally able to get my words out I told her that I could not take life anymore. Life was getting too hard. I told her that there was no way I could go to my job because I was already an emotional wreck and I knew with the nit picking I experienced on a daily basis from my manager would only make things worse. Normally I would go into work and force a smile and a positive attitude all day despite whatever I had going on in my personal life, but this day I just could not do it. My mother told me to take the day off and just call to let my boss know that I could not make it in. I did as she requested suggested and I knew that it was what I needed. There was so much going on and I barely had time to process one thing before something else surfaced. I turned around and went home with my babies.

It was as if my babies knew that I needed that day to ease my mind. They were normally active, up playing and climbing all over me, but that day they slept peacefully for most of the day. I changed into my pajamas and laid on the couch in the living room; face ashy and eyes puffy from crying so much. I sat in the living room, free of any noise or electronics and I felt a sense of peace come over me. The next day when I returned to work. I was called into the office after working the entire day. My manager explained that I had violated the attendance policy and they had no other choice but to terminate me. Deep down I felt a sense of relief...of peace or a feeling that felt more like peace. After the panic attack that I'd had the previous morning, I knew that my mind and my body needed rest. I knew my time was up with that company. In all honesty, I had been feeling in my spirit the day was coming soon because there was something else I was supposed to be doing. But my worries over our current financial situation were clearly at the top of my priorities. We had just gotten a new vehicle and we were already struggling to get by with both of our incomes and now we were going to have to manage with one. I knew that the test was about to get so much harder than it already was, but I also knew God was removing me from my job for a reason.

My manager made the statement that indicating how relieved I looked when they were letting me go. My guess is she was expecting me to cry or be dramatic about being fired, but the situation was out of my control and she had no idea what other battles I had been facing so she wouldn't have and I had no desire to make her understand; therefore, I didn't try and if I tried to explain. I responded to her statement by saying I know that God has a plan. I went around gathered my belongings and said my goodbyes to my co-workers and left with a smile.

Just like with my other trials, my husband was supportive despite our marital problems. I expected nothing less from him because he was always the positive thinker in all aspects of our life together. The free time that I had during the day, allowed my husband and I the much-needed time to spend with each other one on one to work on our marriage. Since the childcare was already paid up for the rest of the month we kept our girls in school and used the time to date, workout, and do other things that we enjoyed doing together. I was beginning to see with every situation we face in life, there are two different perspectives, positive or negative. There is some positive in every situation. Sometimes it is easier to recognize only the negative in our trials, but when we seek the positives…the blessings are revealed to us in blinding Technicolor.

Not only did the time allow me to spend more time with my husband; but it also allowed me to spend more times with my kids once we finally took them out of school. More time getting back to doing things I enjoy and most of all, the time to really focus and rely on God. Even though we were suddenly dependent on one income, we were getting by better than we were when I was employed. I still wanted to help my family get where we needed to be. I was denied unemployment because my manager submitted a statement stating she thought I was trying to make them terminate me simply because I said God has a plan. I was angry because I had two children who had needs and she was doing everything she could to jeopardize any chances of me getting my unemployment benefits to help my husband provide for our family. I asked God to help me forgive her and not harbor any hatred in my heart for what she was doing.

Sitting at the kitchen table, trying to figure out how to make a meal out of the few items in the refrigerator and the canned vegetables in the cabinet, I thought about how hateful and nasty my manager had been to me over the years I worked with her. I also thought about going into her office and telling her just what her mean and hateful ways was doing to my family, but I never did. I just figured out a meal and hoped my family would eat it. There were days I wished I had called HR for the harassment and other unethical practices she did like my co-workers told me to do. None of that was going to solve or change anything and although I was angry and frustrated; it wasn't in my character to do or cause harm to anyone... despite what they did to me. Despite the upheaval taking place in my life, I continued to draw closer to God and started reading the Bible daily, journaling, and going to church every Sunday.

Not even a month after I lost my job, we received a letter informing us that our lease was up and we would not be able to renew it due to the fact we had been late on the rent month after month. It was a difficult realization and we were disappointed that we were going to have to move and start all over again. We knew that the search for a new place would be hard since we were just in the same predicament earlier that year. Being a part was not an option; separating from each other once again was not what we wanted to do. For about 3 weeks, we stayed at a family member's house together as a family, but it was more convenient for everyone involved for us to stay separately at our parent's houses… *again*. Together my husband and I planned to give ourselves two months to make the living situations work and had hopes of having our own place by then in Charlotte, NC.

My husband and I traveled to Charlotte at least twice a week, going to interviews, job fairs, and house hunting…doing everything in preparation for what we hoped would help us to make a smooth and successful transition to the state. We were more motivated than ever to turn our finances and living arrangement around and rebuild our lives. We were so focused on making the moves we wanted to make, we didn't stop much to think about if it was the right time to move. Our hopes of having a smooth transition to Charlotte went down the drain. The deadline that we gave ourselves passed and there we were still trying to find our way out of our parent's house. When it rains it pours, but thank God for His umbrella of grace.

Chapter 7

God had a much bigger plan than I ever imagined. I had no idea what I was doing, I just knew I had to do something.

The year was coming to an end. I should have been getting excited about enjoying the upcoming holiday festivities and creating memories with my family; instead, I was lying awake in bed, pondering on what the next year would be like. It was after midnight and everyone else in the house was asleep. My brain was clouded with thoughts of what I could do to ensure my family did not have another year like this past one. I prayed the same prayer I had prayed many times before,

> "Lord I pray that you will show me your will for my life. I know that this is not your best for me. I want what you want for my family and me. Please guide me in the direction that you need me to go. My family is in desperate need of a breakthrough."

How did I end up at my parent's house once again; now married with two babies, no job, and no home? A chilling feeling came over me and tears started streaming down my cheeks. *"God whatever it is you want me to do, I will do it."* In the middle of my crucible, God began to speak to me. He revealed to me my destiny and what I needed to do to get there. My thoughts shifted from what I was worried about to the spiritual exchange I shared with God. Spiritual leaders always say if you listen hard enough you can hear God. To hear God, I had to get quiet. How am I to hear the music if the noise inside my head is louder than the tunes? Similarly, how was I to hear the voice of God, if the chatter in my soul was louder than His voice?

I remembered there had been other times I sat in silence, mind focused only on God and experienced the same voice as if he was there in the room. I compared them to times I spent crying, worrying and stressing while asking God for answers; those were times he seemed so far away. I could not sleep at all that night. I turned on Pandora to Mary Mary's radio to clear my mind of any distractions and focus solely on God, and the assignment and promises he was making clear to me. I heard the voice say *Sister of Sincerity.*

For weeks, I questioned what the assignment was about. *What am I supposed to do with this God?* Truth was, I already knew, but I couldn't understand why God chose me of all people, to carry out this assignment. In those weeks, I wrote a list of the things God placed on my heart.

On the list, I wrote:

- Blog
- Book
- Women's group
- Counselor/life coach

I found every excuse I could possibly find to talk myself out of having to do the work. *Lord, who is going to care about anything I say? How am I supposed to empower others when my life is a mess? Lord you know I am too shy to talk in front of people? I don't know where to start.* I kept hearing "just write." and "just start". God was showing me just what to do, but fear and doubt consumed me. Who was I to think my words, my voice, my story could make a difference? No matter what I did during the day, the assignment was all I could think about. Thoughts of how to get started kept me up at night. After about 2 weeks of not being able to sleep or think about anything other than what God was calling me to do, I surrendered.

I turned on the computer and researched on how to start a blog. In a matter of three hours, I created a website, posted and published my first blog post at 3:00 a.m. The pressure that had been weighing heavily on me since God spoke to me to do these things was suddenly lifted.

Before returning to bed I looked over my work and said a prayer before posting it on my personal social media accounts. After finally stepping out on faith and following the calling I had been fighting for weeks, I was able to sleep peacefully again; like a little baby with a full tummy and after a warm bath.

When I woke up, I was surprised to see my notifications were flooded with people sharing my blog post and website. I was overwhelmed and beaming. Family, friends, and people I didn't *even* know personally were enjoying my very first blog post. Many of them encouraged me to continue posting.

"You've got something special girl, keep posting!" One message said. I scrolled through in amazement and another said, *"You have no idea how much I needed that. Thank you."* Every week I shared encouraging blog post and every week more and more individuals shared with me how my words made a difference in their lives. Women messaged me privately for prayer, encouragement, and advice. I knew God had a much bigger plan than I ever imagined. I had no idea what I was doing, I just knew I had to do something. I reflected on how my life was leading up to that point and after 26 years it all made sense to me. God was using me and everything I had been through from the time I was 10 years old, hating my

own existence, to the teen that searched for love that only God could give, to the young adult trying to figure life out while experiencing death, to being the wife and mother that just couldn't seem to get it right while just trying to create a better life for my family...He would use all of it for His purpose. He would take my mess and turn it into my message.

There was a time I felt like God was taking everything away from me as a form of punishment for my mistakes. It made sense why God allowed me to lose so many things and why He removed me from certain places. God was only preparing me for what He called me to do. He stripped my life of things I thought I needed to survive, so He could prove to me he was all I needed from the beginning. He was teaching me to trust and rely on him more than man or worldly possessions. Everything I had been through, positioned me to help others who may have faced the same or similar situations. *Sister of Sincerity* made sense. For me to be sincere in helping my sisters and brothers, I had to experience what it was like to go through. I wanted everyone to know that I understood what it was like to struggle with loving my own identity, to feel lonely in a world full of people, to want to end my own life to make everyone else's easier, to give my heart to someone only to have it broken, to face depression year after year, to lose loved ones, to lose everything I owned... to fail.

The strength and wisdom I gained were enough to pull the broken pieces back together to form a beautiful masterpiece. When I felt the pieces come together I knew I had found my purpose.

God confirmed that I was indeed walking in my purpose. Every conversation I had, every video I clicked, and even small reminders daily confirmed my purpose. Even through the death of my cousin, Dedrick God was confirming my calling.

***

Dedrick and I grew up side by side, practically in the same house; one always at the other's house or both at our grandmother's house. As we grew older our bond remained strong, like we were as kids, when we would walk to each other's house before we could wash our faces and get the crust out of our eyes. We played Mario cart on the Nintendo 64 every day until somebody made us go find something to do outside. Between my junior and senior years of college, Dedrick moved in with me. He was always a hard worker but was tired of the same scenery every day. I loved his company, so without hesitation, I suggested he transfer his job and move in with me. Our talks usually consisted of constant laughter, encouragement and sharing memories of Brittney.

Brittney's passing affected both of tremendously; however, we helped one another get through it by constantly checking on each other and visiting her grave site together. We both had a really hard time but knew the best way to pay tribute to her was to enjoy life and live out our dreams. We wanted to make her proud. Dedrick was the one family member that stood close to me and constantly checked in on me, the same way Brittney did. He always reminded me that we had each other to go through life with. I found comfort in knowing I was not alone. I was so proud of the strength we gained together and how we uplifted each other through such tragedy. I looked forward to being able to grow old and one-day share stories of our childhood and how we pushed through a tough time in our lives and still became successful. Life continues to teach me one simple lesson; it does not go according to our plans.

February 18, 2016, I was stretched across the bed in what used to be my brother's room at our parent's house. I was just beginning to drift off into a deep sleep when Josh came rushing in calling my name.

"Quietta wake up." *Man, what do he want, the sleep was just getting good.* I was trying to get a nap in before I had to get back to my babies. *Maybe if I pretend I don't hear him he'll go away.*

"Quietta, wake up!" This time I noticed a dull sound in his voice. It wasn't like the times he woke me up out of my sleep just to annoy me. I sat up slowly and stretched.

"You up?" He asked.

"Yeah, What's up?"

"Dedrick just died, man."

For a few seconds, everything around me seemed to stand still.

"Huh?" I said obviously confused.

"Did you hear me? Dedrick is gone?!" I could tell he was waiting for me to break down, but in my head, it wasn't real. I was still half asleep and I wasn't sure if I was dreaming or not. I heard the door in the living room shut. It was my aunt Mary Jane.

"I'm here with her now. Josh is here too." She was on the phone with my mother. "Okay, I'll call you back."

"Y'all alright?" She asked. My head was spinning now. I rubbed my temples.

"They transported his body to the hospital. Everybody is going up there now. I'm about to ride up there too." My aunt's phone rang again. It was my mother calling.

"No, she's not okay. She's not saying anything at all. I don't think it hit her yet."

It really hadn't hit me yet. I was seriously in a state of disbelief, maybe even shock. I had just seen and talked to him the day before. He was supposed to come visit this week. There was no way he was gone. Dedrick's health had gotten really bad the previous year, but by the grace of God, he fought through it. He battled health issues from birth, but he was strong. He promised he would keep fighting. I simply did not believe he was gone. My aunt made sure my brother was not going to leave me there alone, and she left to go to the hospital. I went to the bathroom, my knees trembled with each step. I sat on the toilet and prayed. *God, please don't let him be gone. Please, God, I can't go through this again.* The truth was starting to set in.

Then suddenly the phone rang. It was my aunt calling. My brother answered. "He got a heartbeat!" By that time, hours had passed since they first told me he passed. I ran out the bathroom almost tripping over my own feet. "They got a heartbeat?" I asked in amazement. My brother was just as shocked "She said they found a heartbeat." It had to be a miracle. I immediately went into prayer first thanking God he was still alive then praying he would make it through the same way he had done before. That night was a sleepless one. Every time the phone rang my heart sank and skipped a beat. I could barely function the next day partially because of the lack of sleep and partially because my mind was on him.

The morning of February 19th Travis and I got the kids ready and headed to town to run errands. On the car ride to the bank, I looked back and noticed that Talayna was covering her face and peeping at the passenger side door where I was sitting.

"Mommy I'm scared of that thing right there in front of you."

"What thing," I asked. There was nothing there. *I knew she was seeing whatever she was seeing with her spiritual eye and it put me on full alert.*

"It's right there in the corner." She said pointing toward the front, but still averting her eyes. An eerie feeling settled over me. I had never seen my daughter react that way and immediately, thoughts of Dedrick flooded my mind; drowning me in memories and fear.

I sat in the bank awaiting the banker to complete my transaction. The transaction was taking a while so I decided to pull up my social media account to keep me entertained. Something I really wish I had not done. My body went weak and my fingers went limp dropping the phone in my lap. Sadly, the first thing that I saw was R.I.P Dedrick. It felt as though the world around me just stopped moving. A huge lump formed in the center of my throat. My entire body shook as I used every bit of strength I had to keep my composure and not break down in front of a bunch of strangers.

My phone rang and I knew whatever I was going to hear on the other end was only going to confirm that he was really gone this time. Thankfully the banker was finishing up my transaction. My knees trembled and I struggled to not fall as I walked outside to the car where my husband and kids were waiting, trying to avoid eye contact with anyone along the way. I got into the passenger side turned to Travis and told him "Dedrick died." Then submitted to the pain I tried so hard to mask. My tears that day were from the thought that we had talked so many times about how we were going to grow old together and make Brittney proud, and wondering if he had been happy before he died. A day later, while lying in bed at my parent's house, is when it really hit me... he was not *here* on this Earth anymore and I would never have the chance to talk and laugh with him again. My chest tightened and I became so frightened I could not calm myself down. It was almost like I forgot how to breathe. Panting and crying hysterically, I ran around the corner to where my mom was sitting, watching T.V. "Ma... I... can't... breathe." I panted out. Trying to breathe through the pain in my chest.

"Calm down Quietta, you got to breathe." She kept telling me to breathe, but I couldn't. "Here, drink some water." My chest continues to rise and fall rapidly. My mother was beginning to panic herself. "Quietta What's wrong. Calm down. What happened?" Her voice a mixture of fear and frustration.

"He's... Gone. Ma—" I said through hampered breaths. My mother tried everything she could to calm me down, but being a mother myself now, I understand it is never easy to watch your kids hurt. I guess seeing me hurt and not being able to take that pain away was overwhelming and I knew she was hurting as well. She yelled for my father to come in.

"What's going on?" He asked.

"She got upset about Dedrick"

My dad sat next to me. "Hey, calm down. I know it hurts...Dedrick meant a lot to all of us. He fought a long and hard battle, but he is in a better place now." My father never sympathized with me or comforted me like this before. His words were genuine and sincere. "You know Dedrick would not want you to worry yourself sick. He lived a good life. He served his purpose."

Out of everything my father said, it was those last few words that stuck with me. Once I calmed down. I sat in the room and reflected on Dedrick's life. My dad was right, he had served his purpose. He was always helping someone in any way he could. It gave him so much joy to put a smile on other people's faces. I know God was pleased with his willingness to serve. In a way, losing my cousin saved my life. The strength and determination I gained were more than I ever knew I could possess. I made a promise to live for God and fulfill my purpose. *That* would be my tribute to Dedrick. I wanted to always have the feeling of knowing I can help someone on this journey of life and be remembered for fulfilling my purpose. Instead of looking at the rough points in my life as downfalls, I began to look for ways to help others who may be going through the same thing.

Spoonful of wisdom

Sometimes what we go through in life is not all about us. Sometimes God allows us to go through things to learn how to grow through them so we can teach and guide others in the right direction. Obedience was the first and most important step in doing what God called me to do. He made it clear to me what He wanted but it was up to me to choose to do the work. The more obedient I became the more He revealed to me. Once I realized what God's plan was for me, it quickly became a passion for me to help God's people and a passion for me to live for God and please Him in all ways I possibly could. God broke me down to help me to find my purpose. He worked on me from the inside out. Negativity, doubt, and fear no longer exist. I've learned to preserve my spirit and focus only on things that are going to help me to grow, glorify God and live out my purpose.

It was an internal change that had to happen; Once I accepted the changes, my life and my relationships with the people around me changed. Through lots of praying and spiritual fasting, my mindset changed from being fearful of taking chances to being fearless, courageous and confident in my gifts. I was known for being quiet my whole life, a word that became part of who I was for the wrong reasons, but I began to use my voice to speak and share my story to uplift and encourage others. On my journey to fulfilling my purpose, I grew closer to God, learned valuable life lessons, and gained the confidence and love I had been longing for throughout my life.

At times I worried about if I could continue what I started. I was not in any position to encourage others because I needed encouragement myself, but when God gives you a vision he also gives provision. Life threw some hard balls and I still get beat down and defeated but instead of staying down I remember how God used everything I was and made me who I am today to help others. I know whatever life brings now, it is all for a purpose much greater than what I or anyone else can see. Many people live full lives never finding or fulfilling their purpose, so for me to be living out my purpose is a huge accomplishment and the ultimate goal fulfilled.

My purpose is to help others find and fulfill their purpose. I chose to write this book because there is someone who needs to know that we were not born with bad luck, the odds may seem like they are against us, but it is only because we were created for something far greater than our eyes can see. I encourage those who are in the pursuit of purpose to trust where God has you and where He is taking you. Remain faithful to His words and stand on His promises. Even when you find it hard to believe, remember for everything He allows you to go through... He will also help you to grow through and it will all make sense when God reveals to you what your purpose is. Your spirit may be broken, your heart may be broken, your whole life may become broken, but the pieces will eventually come together exactly how they're supposed to. All those broken pieces coming together to reveal God's purpose for your life...what an amazing gift.

~prayer~
Dear God

Life hasn't always been easy, but I thank you for everything you have allowed me to go through that got me to where I am now. I thank you for every person I have encountered along the way. I am now able to see myself as you see me now and I understand my life has always had meaning. At times I felt broken, but you have managed to put each piece back together and create something more beautiful than I could have ever imagined. My prayer is that you will continue to prepare me for my greatest purpose.

Amen